The Supporters' Guide to Premiership & Football League Clubs 1997

EDITOR
John Robinson

Thirteenth Edition

British Library Cataloguing in Publication Data
A catalogue record for this book is available from the British Library

ISBN 0-947808-70-1

Copyright © 1996, SOCCER BOOK PUBLISHING LTD. (01472 696226)
72 St. Peter's Avenue, Cleethorpes, N.E. Lincolnshire, DN35 8HU, England

Printed by Redwood Books, Kennet House, Kennet Way, Trowbridge, Wilts.

CONTENTS

FOREWORD

We are indebted to the staffs of the clubs featured in this guide for their cooperation and also to Michael Robinson (page layouts), Ceri Sampson (cover artwork) and Kevin Norminton (photos).

When using this guide, please note that 'child' concessions generally include senior citizens also. A number of clubs had not set their 1996/97 Season admission prices when we completed the guide and where this was the case we have shown 1995/96 price information.

Disabled Supporters' information is once again included in the guide and, to ensure that facilities are not overstretched, we recommend that disabled fans pre-book wherever possible.

Regular purchasers of the guide will notice that we have used new ground photos to illustrate the incredible developments which have taken place over the last 3 or 4 years. However, ground moves and redevelopment are continuing apace and travelling fans may find that away sections and prices change during the course of the 1996/97 season.

Finally, we would like to wish our readers a happy and safe spectating season.

John Robinson
EDITOR

THE
NATIONAL FOOTBALL
STADIA
OF
BRITAIN

WELSH NATIONAL STADIUM

Re-opened for Football: 31st May 1989
Location: Cardiff City Centre, Cardiff
Telephone: (01222) 390111 (Ground)
Telephone: (01222) 372325 (F.A. of Wales)
Address: The National Ground, Cardiff
Arms Park, Westgate Street, Cardiff, Wales
Pitch Size: 110 × 69 yards

Ground Capacity: 51,374
Seating Capacity: 42,355
(40,240 for Football Matches)
Note: This stadium will be closed late in
1996 for redevelopment and at the time of
going to press the alternate venues are not
known

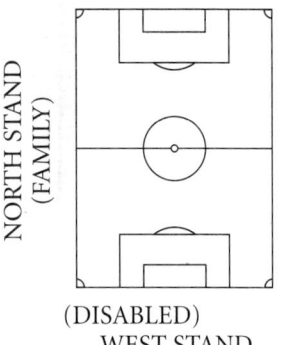

EAST TERRACE
(Not used for Soccer Matches)

NORTH STAND (FAMILY)

SOUTH STAND (FAMILY)

(DISABLED)
WEST STAND

GENERAL INFORMATION

Car Parking: City Centre car parks
Coach Parking: By Police direction
Nearest Railway Station: 5-10 minutes walk
Nearest Bus Station: 5 minutes walk
Nearest Police Station: Cardiff Centre
Police Force: South Wales
Police Telephone Nº: (01222) 222111

GROUND INFORMATION

Away Supporters' Entrances & Sections:
Lower Tier of North and South Stands

DISABLED INFORMATION

Wheelchairs: Accommodated in the disabled
section – North side of the West Stand – spaces for
24 wheelchairs
Disabled Toilets: Yes

ADMISSION INFO (1996/97 PRICES)

Adult Seating: £6.00 – £20.00
Child Seating: Half-price in the Family Enclosures
Programme Price: £2.00
FAX Number: (01222) 343961
Note: Prices vary depending on the opponents and
type of game

Travelling Supporters' Information:
Routes: Exit M4 at Junction 29 and take A48(M) following signs for Cardiff City Centre (via A470). Use the City
Centre Public car parks; From Cardiff Central Railway Station: Proceed past the Bus Station, cross Wood Street
and turn down Westgate Street (alongside the back of the Royal Hotel).

WEMBLEY STADIUM

Opened: 1923	**Record Attendance:** 100,000
Location: Wembley, Middlesex HA9 0DW	**Pitch Size:** 115 × 75 yards
Telephone: Box Office (0181) 900-1234	**Ground Capacity:** 80,000
Telephone: Admin. (0181) 902-8833	**Seating Capacity:** 80,000
FAX Number: (0181) 903-4818	

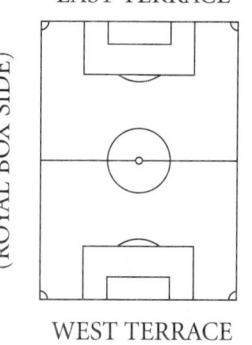

(PLAYERS TUNNEL END)
EAST TERRACE

OLYMPIC WAY & TWIN TOWERS (ROYAL BOX SIDE)

SOUTH STAND

WEST TERRACE
(STADIUM OFFICE END)

GENERAL INFORMATION
Guided Tours Available: (0181) 902-8833
(extension 3346) for details
Car Parking: Car park for over 7,000 vehicles
Coach Parking: Car park at Stadium
Nearest Railway Stations: Wembley Park, Wembley
Central, Wembley Complex (5-10 minutes walk)
Nearest Police Station: Mobile Unit in front of
Twin Towers
Police Telephone Nº: (0181) 903-4818

GROUND INFORMATION
Location of Family Area: North Stand

DISABLED INFORMATION
Wheelchairs: Limited facilities available
Disabled Toilets: Yes

ADMISSION INFO (1995/96 PRICES)
Admission £12.00 – £30.00; depending on the game
and ground position. Also a £1 per seat booking fee
(**Accompanied Children – half-price in family
enclosure**)

HAMPDEN STADIUM

Opened: 1903
Location: In the 'Mount Florida' area of Glasgow, South East of the River Clyde
Telephone: (0141) 632-1275 (Admin.)
FAX Number: (0141) 636-1612
Address: Hampden Park, Mount Florida, Glasgow   G42 9BA

Pitch Size: 115 × 75 yards
Record Attendance: 150,239 (Scotland vs England 17th April 1937)
Ground Capacity: 34,000
Seating Capacity: 34,000
When development complete – 60,000

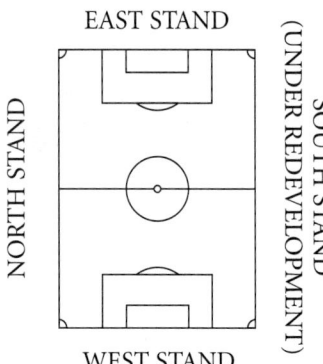

EAST STAND

NORTH STAND

SOUTH STAND (UNDER REDEVELOPMENT)

WEST STAND

GENERAL INFORMATION

Car Parking: Car park for 1,200 vehicles
Coach Parking: Car park at Stadium
Nearest Railway Stations: Mount Florida and Kings Park (both 5 minutes walk)
Nearest Police Station: Aikenhead Road, Glasgow
Police Telephone Nº: (0141) 422-1113

DISABLED INFORMATION

Wheelchairs: Accommodated in temporary disabled spectators section in front of the North Stand
Disabled Toilets: None during redevelopment
The Blind: Personal commentaries

Travelling Supporters' Information:
Routes: From the South: Take the A724 to the Cambuslang Road and at Eastfield branch left into Main Street and follow through Burnhill Street and Westmuir Place into Prospecthill Road. Turn left into Aikenhead Road and right into Mount Annan for Kinghorn Drive and the Stadium; From the West: Take the A77 Fenwick Road, through Kilmarnock Road into Pollokshaws Road then turn right into Langside Avenue. Pass through Battle Place to Battlefield Road and turn left into Cathcart Road. Turn right into Letherby Drive, right into Carmunnock Road and 1st left into Mount Annan Drive for the Stadium; From the North and East; Exit M8 at Junction 15 and passing the Infirmary on the left, proceed into High Street and cross the Albert Bridge into Crown Street. Join Cathcart Road and proceed South until it becomes Carmunnock Road. Turn left into Mount Annan Drive and left again into Kinghorn Drive for the Stadium.

The F.A. Carling Premiership

Founded
1992

Address
16 Lancaster Gate, London   W2 3LW

Phone
(0171) 402-7151

The Nationwide Football League

Founded
1888

Address
Lytham St. Annes, Lancashire   FY8 1JG

Phone
(01253) 729421

ARSENAL FC

Founded: 1886 (**Entered League:** 1893)
Former Names: Royal Arsenal (1886-91);
Woolwich Arsenal (1891-1914)
Nickname: 'Gunners'
Ground: Arsenal Stadium, Avenell Road,
Highbury, London, N5 1BU
Record Attendance: 73,295 (9/3/35)

Colours: Shirts – Red with White Sleeves
Shorts – White
Telephone N°: (0171) 226-0304
Ticket Office: (0171) 354-5404
Fax Number: (0171) 226-0329
Pitch Size: 110 × 71 yards
Ground Capacity: 38,300 (All seats)

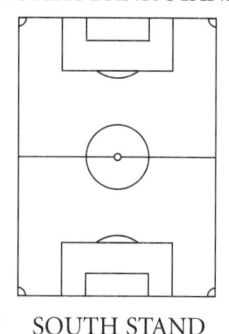

(GILLESPIE ROAD)
NORTH BANK STAND

WEST STAND
Highbury Hill Turnstiles

EAST STAND
AVENELL ROAD

SOUTH STAND

GENERAL INFORMATION

Supporters Club: c/o Barry Baker, 154 St. Thomas's
Road, Finsbury Park, London N4
Telephone N°: (0171) 226-1627
Car Parking: Street Parking
Coach Parking: Drayton Park (N5)
Nearest Railway Stat'n: Drayton Park/Finsbury Park
Nearest Tube Station: Arsenal (Piccadilly)
Club Shop: At Ground
Opening Times: Weekdays 9.30-5.00; Saturday
Matchdays 1.00pm onwards
Telephone N°: (0171) 226-9562
Postal Sales: Yes
Nearest Police Stat'n: 284 Hornsey Road, Holloway
Police Telephone N°: (0171) 263-9090

GROUND INFORMATION

Away Supporters' Entrances & Sections:
South Stand – Blocks 17 & 18

ADMISSION INFO (1996/97 PRICES)

Adult Seating: £12.00 – £28.00
Child Seating: £7.00 (members only, Family Stand)
Programme Price: £1.50

DISABLED INFORMATION

Wheelchairs: 20 spaces in total for Home and Away
fans in the disabled section, Lower Tier East Stand
Helpers: One helper admitted per wheelchair
Prices: Free of charge for Disabled and Helpers
Disabled Toilets: 3 Available in the South Stand,
one available in the Lower East 'H' Block
Commentaries are available for the blind
Are Bookings Necessary: Yes
Contact: (0171) 226-0304

Travelling Supporters' Information:
Routes: From North: Exit M1 at Junction 2 following City signs. After Holloway Road Station (6¼ miles) 3rd
left into Drayton Park, after ¾ mile right into Aubert Park and 2nd left into Avenell Road. From South: From
London Bridge follow signs to Bank of England then Angel. Right at traffic lights to Highbury Roundabout (1
mile), into Holloway Road then 3rd right into Drayton Park (then as North). From West: Exit M4 Junction 1
towards Chiswick (A315), left after 1 mile (A40) to M41 then A40(M) to A501 Ring Road turn left Angel to
Highbury Roundabout (then as South).

ASTON VILLA FC

Founded: 1874 (**Entered League:** 1888)
Former Names: None
Nickname: 'The Villans'; 'Villa'
Ground: Villa Park, Trinity Road,
Birmingham B6 6HE
Record Attendance: 76,588 (2/3/46)

Colours: Shirts – Claret with Blue Sleeves
Shorts – White
Telephone Nº: (0121) 327-2299
Ticket Office: (0121) 327-5353
Fax Number: (0121) 322-2107
Pitch Size: 115 × 75 yards
Ground Capacity: 39,339 (All seats)

GENERAL INFORMATION

Supporters Club: c/o Club's Commercial Dept.
Telephone Nº: (0121) 327-5399
Car Parking: Aston Villa Leisure Centre Car Park,
Aston Hall Road
Coach Parking: Opposite Ground
Nearest Railway Stat'n: Witton or Aston (5 minutes
walk)
Nearest Bus Station: Birmingham Centre
Club Shop: At Ground
Opening Times: Weekdays / Matchdays 9.30 – 5.00
(closes during the match)
Telephone Nº: (0121) 327-2800
Postal Sales: Yes
Nearest Police Stat'n: Queen's Road, Aston (½ mile)
Police Telephone Nº: (0121) 322-6010

GROUND INFORMATION

Away Supporters' Entrances & Sections:
Witton End – 'R' Block

ADMISSION INFO (1996/97 PRICES)

Adult Seating: £14.00 – £17.00
Child Seating: £6.00 – £9.00
Programme Price: £1.50

DISABLED INFORMATION

Wheelchairs: 56 spaces in total for Home and Away
fans in a special section – Trinity Road Stand &
Holte End
Helpers: By letter of request of disabled – One per
disabled fan
Prices: At club's discretion for the disabled. Helpers
full price
Disabled Toilets: Trinity Road Stand & Holte End
Commentaries are available by arrangement
Are Bookings Necessary: Yes
Contact: (0121) 327-2299

Travelling Supporters' Information:
Routes: From all parts: Exit M6 at Junction 6 (Spaghetti Junction). Follow signs for Birmingham (NE). Take the
4th exit at the roundabout onto the A38 (M) signposted Aston. After ½ mile, turn right into Aston Hall Road.
Bus Services: Service 7 from Corporation Street to Witton Square. Also some specials.

BARNET FC

Founded: 1888 (**Entered League:** 1991)
Former Names: Barnet Alston
Nickname: 'Bees'
Ground: Underhill Stadium, Westcombe
Drive, Barnet, Herts. EN5 2BE
Record Attendance: 11,026 (1952)
Pitch Size: 113 × 72 yards

Colours: Shirts – Amber w/ Black Collar
Shorts – Black w/ Amber Trim
Telephone Nº: (0181) 441-6932
Ticket Office: (0181) 441-6932
Fax Number: (0181) 447-0655
Ground Capacity: 3,887
Seating Capacity: 1,773

SOUTH STAND
(Away)

PRIORY GROVE

EAST TERRACE

BARNET LANE
MAIN STAND

NORTH TERRACE

GENERAL INFORMATION

Supporters Club: c/o Club Shop
Telephone Nº: –
Car Parking: Street Parking and High Barnet Underground Car Park
Coach Parking: By Police Direction
Nearest Railway Stat'n: New Barnet (1½ miles)
Nearest Tube Station: High Barnet (Northern) (5 minutes walk)
Club Shop: At Ground
Opening Times: Tuesdays, Thursday, Fridays & Matchdays – 11.00am to 5.00pm
Telephone Nº: (0181) 441-6932
Postal Sales: Yes
Nearest Police Stat'n: Barnet (¼ mile)
Police Telephone Nº: (0181) 200-2212

GROUND INFORMATION

Away Supporters' Entrances & Sections:
Entrances in Priory Grove for the South Stand

ADMISSION INFO (1996/97 PRICES)

Adult Standing: £7.00 (Members £5.00 North Tce.)
Adult Seating: £12.00 (£8.00 in the Family Stand)
Child Standing: £3.50 (Members free North Tce.)
Child Seating: £6.00 (£4.00 in the Family Stand)
(Family Tickets are also available)
Programme Price: £1.20
Note: Concessionary prices are for members only

DISABLED INFORMATION

Wheelchairs: 12 spaces in total for Home and Away fans in the Main Stand – Barnet Lane Entrance
Helpers: One helper admitted per wheelchair
Prices: Contact the club for details
Disabled Toilets: One available in the Social Club
Are Bookings Necessary: Yes
Contact: (0181) 441-6932

Travelling Supporters' Information:
Routes: The ground is situated off the Great North Road (A1000) at the foot of Barnet Hill near to the junction with Station Road (A110). Barnet Lane is on the west of the A1000 next to the Cricket Ground.

BARNSLEY FC

Founded: 1887 (**Entered League:** 1898)	**Colours:** Shirts – Red
Former Names: Barnsley St. Peter's	Shorts – White
Nickname: 'Tykes'; 'Colliers'; 'Reds'	**Telephone Nº:** (01226) 211211
Ground: Oakwell Ground, Grove Street,	**Ticket Office:** (01226) 211211
Barnsley S71 1ET	**Fax Number:** (01226) 211444
Record Attendance: 40,255 (15/2/36)	**Pitch Size:** 110 × 75 yards
	Ground Capacity: 19,034 (All seats)

SPION KOP SEATING
(Away)

DISABLED STAND

WEST STAND (Away)

EAST STAND

ORA STAND

GENERAL INFORMATION

Supporters Club: Mr. A. Bloore, c/o Barnsley FC
Telephone Nº: (01302) 883481
Car Parking: Queen's Ground Car Park (adjacent)
Coach Parking: Queen's Ground Car Park
Nearest Railway Stat'n: Barnsley Exchange (5 mins. walk)
Nearest Bus Station: Barnsley Exchange
Club Shop: At Ground
Opening Times: Weekdays 9.30-5.00; Saturday Matchdays 9.00-5.30; Other Saturdays 9.00-12.00
Telephone Nº: (01226) 211211
Postal Sales: Yes (Also Credit Card Sales)
Nearest Police Stat'n: Churchfields, Barnsley
Police Telephone Nº: (01226) 206161

GROUND INFORMATION

Away Supporters' Entrances & Sections:
West Stand and Spion Kop

ADMISSION INFO (1996/97 PRICES)

Adult Seating: £10.00 – £12.50
Child Seating: £6.00 – £6.50
Note: Concessions available on a reciprocal basis on pre-purchased tickets
Programme Price: £1.50

DISABLED INFORMATION

Wheelchairs: 120 spaces in total for Home and Away fans in the Disabled Stand, situated to the left of the West Stand
Helpers: Admitted depending on room available
Prices: Free for the disabled, £8.00 for helpers in the Disabled Stand. Alternatively Pre-booked places are available in the Disabled Section of the Ora Stand at £6.00 for both the disabled and helpers
Disabled Toilets: Adjacent to the Disabled Stand
Commentaries are available for the blind
Are Bookings Necessary: Usually not
Contact: (01226) 211211

Travelling Supporters' Information:
Routes: From All Parts: Exit M1 at Junction 37 and follow the 'Football Ground' signs to the ground (2 miles).

BIRMINGHAM CITY FC

Founded: 1875 (**Entered League:** 1892) **Former Names:** Small Heath Alliance FC (1875-88); Small Heath FC (1888-1905); Birmingham FC (1905-1945) **Nickname:** 'Blues' **Ground:** St. Andrew's, St. Andrew's Street, Birmingham B9 4NH	**Record Attendance:** 68,844 (11/2/39) **Colours:** Shirts – Blue Shorts – White **Telephone Nº:** (0121) 772-0101 **Ticket Office:** (0121) 772-0101 **Fax Number:** (0121) 766-7866 **Pitch Size:** 115 × 75 yards **Ground Capacity:** 24,796 (All seats)

TILTON ROAD STAND

ST. ANDREW'S STREET STAND

CATTELL ROAD STAND

(Away)
RAILWAY STAND

GENERAL INFORMATION

Supporters Club: c/o Linda Goodman, 69 Malmesbury Road, Small Heath, Birmingham
Telephone Nº: (0121) 773-5088
Car Parking: Street Parking
Coach Parking: Coventry Road
Nearest Railway Stat'n: Birmingham New Street or Birmingham Moor Street (20 minutes walk)
Nearest Bus Station: Digbeth
Club Shops: At Dale End and Cattell Road
Opening Times: Monday to Saturday 9.00am to 5.30pm (Open until 7.00pm on Thursdays)
Telephone Nº: (0121) 753-1997
Postal Sales: Yes
Nearest Police Stat'n: Bordesley Green (½ mile)
Police Telephone Nº: (0121) 772-1166

GROUND INFORMATION

Away Supporters' Entrances & Sections:
Railway Stand End

ADMISSION INFO (1996/97 PRICES)

Adult Seating: £10.00 – £16.00
Child Seating: £5.00 – £8.00
Note: Prices vary according to match category and the position in the ground
Programme Price: £1.50

DISABLED INFORMATION

Wheelchairs: Spaces available in the Cattell Road Stand and Family Stand.
Helpers: One helper admitted per wheelchair
Prices: £5.00 for disabled fans, £7.00 for helpers
Disabled Toilets: Available in the Cattell Road and Family Stands
Are Bookings Necessary: Yes
Contact: (0121) 772-0101

Travelling Supporters' Information:
Routes: From All Parts: Exit M6 at Junction 6 and take the A38 (M) (Aston Expressway). Leave at 2nd exit then take first exit at roundabout along the Dartmouth Middleway. After 1¼ miles turn left into St. Andrew's Street.
Bus Services: Service 97 from Birmingham; Services 98 & 99 from Digbeth.

14

BLACKBURN ROVERS FC

Founded: 1875 (**Entered League:** 1888)
Former Names: None
Nickname: 'Rovers'; 'Blues & Whites'
Ground: Ewood Park, Blackburn,
Lancashire   BB2 4JF
Record Attendance: 61,783 (2/3/29)

Colours: Shirts – Blue and White Halves
    Shorts – White
Telephone Nº: (01254) 698888
Ticket Office: (01254) 671666
Fax Number: (01254) 671042
Pitch Size: 117 × 73 yards
Ground Capacity: 31,169 (All seats)

DARWEN END
(Away)

WALKERSTEEL STAND

JACK WALKER STAND

BOLTON ROAD

BLACKBURN END
KIDDER STREET

GENERAL INFORMATION

Supporters Club: Barbara Magee, c/o Ewood Park
Telephone Nº: (01254) 698888
Car Parking: Street Parking (nearby)
Coach Parking: By Police direction
Nearest Railway Stat'n: Blackburn Central (1½ mls)
Nearest Bus Station: Blackburn Central (1½ miles)
Club Shop: At Ground
Opening Times: Weekdays 9.00-5.30; Saturday
Matchdays 9.30-3.00; Sundays 11.00-3.00
Telephone Nº: (01254) 672333
Postal Sales: Yes
Nearest Police Stat'n: Blackburn (2 miles)
Police Telephone Nº: (01254) 51212

GROUND INFORMATION

Away Supporters' Entrances & Sections:
Darwen End

ADMISSION INFO (1996/97 PRICES)

Adult Seating: £15.00 – £19.00
Child Seating: £8.00 – £9.00
Programme Price: £1.50

DISABLED INFORMATION

Wheelchairs: 140 spaces in total for Home and
Away fans in the disabled section, Walkersteel Stand
Helpers: One helper admitted per disabled fan
Prices: Free for the Disabled. Helpers normal prices
Disabled Toilets: Available in the disabled section
Commentaries are available by arrangement for up
to 6 people
Are Bookings Necessary: Yes
Contact: (01254) 698888

Travelling Supporters' Information:
Routes: From North, South and West: Exit M6 at Junction 31, or take the A666. Follow signs for Blackburn then
for Bolton Road and after 1½ miles turn left into Kidder Street; From East: Use the A679 or A677 and follow
signs for Bolton Road – then as above.

Blackpool FC

Founded: 1887 (**Entered League:** 1896)	**Colours:** Shirts – Tangerine
Former Names: Merged with Blackpool	Shorts – Tangerine
St. Johns in 1887	**Telephone Nº:** (01253) 404331
Nickname: 'Seasiders'	**Ticket Office:** (01253) 404331
Ground: Bloomfield Road, Blackpool,	**Fax Number:** (01253) 405011
Lancashire FY1 6JJ	**Pitch Size:** 112 × 74 yards
Record Attendance: 38,098 (17/9/55)	**Ground Capacity:** 10,200
	Seating Capacity: 2,987

SPION KOP
EAST SECTION (Away)
WEST STAND
HENRY STREET
EAST PADDOCK
SOUTH STAND
BLOOMFIELD ROAD

GENERAL INFORMATION

Supporters Club: c/o Colin Johnson, Blackpool Supporters' Club, Bloomfield Road, Blackpool
Telephone Nº: (01253) 46428 (Evenings only 7.00pm-11.00pm)
Car Parking: Car Park at the Ground for 3,000 cars and street parking
Coach Parking: Mecca Car Park (behind Spion Kop)
Nearest Railway Stat'n: Blackpool South (5 mins.)
Nearest Bus Station: Talbot Road (2 miles)
Club Shop: At Ground
Opening Times: Daily from 9.00am to 5.30pm
Telephone Nº: (01253) 404331
Postal Sales: Yes
Nearest Police Stat'n: South Shore, Montague Street, Blackpool
Police Telephone Nº: (01253) 293933

GROUND INFORMATION

Away Supporters' Entrances & Sections:
Spion Kop turnstiles for the Spion Kop and East Paddock North Section

ADMISSION INFO (1996/97 PRICES)

Adult Standing: £8.50
Adult Seating: £10.00 – £11.00
Child Standing: £5.00
Child Seating: £6.50 – £7.50
FAMILY BLOCK: – Various additional discounts
1 Adult + 1 Child   £13.00
2 Adults + 1 Child   £23.00
Programme Price: £1.20

DISABLED INFORMATION

Wheelchairs: 12 spaces in total for Home and Away fans in the disabled area, South Stand
Helpers: One helper admitted per disabled fan
Prices: Free of charge for Disabled and Helpers
Disabled Toilets: None
Commentaries are available for 3 people in the South Stand
Are Bookings Necessary: Yes
Contact: (01253) 404331

Travelling Supporters' Information:
Routes: From All Parts: Exit M6 at Junction 32 onto the M55. Follow signs for the main car parks along the new 'spine' road to the car parks at the side of the ground.

BOLTON WANDERERS FC

Founded: 1874 (**Entered League:** 1888)
Former Names: Christchurch FC (1874-1877)
Nickname: 'Trotters'
Ground: Burnden Park, Manchester Road, Bolton BL3 2QR
Record Attendance: 69,912 (18/2/33)

Colours: Shirts – White
Shorts – Blue
Telephone Nº: (01204) 389200
Ticket Office: (01204) 521101
Fax Number: (01204) 382334
Pitch Size: 113 × 75 yards
Ground Capacity: 20,800
Seating Capacity: 7,850

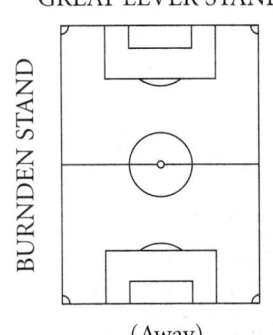

(CROFT LANE)
GREAT LEVER STAND

BURNDEN STAND

MANCHESTER ROAD STAND

(Away)
EMBANKMENT

GENERAL INFORMATION

Supporters Club: c/o P. Entwistle, 21 Woodfield, Bolton
Telephone Nº: –
Car Parking: Rosehill Car Park (nearby)
Coach Parking: Rosehill Car Park, Manchester Road
Nearest Railway Stat'n: Bolton Trinity Street (½ ml)
Nearest Bus Station: Moor Lane, Bolton
Club Shop: At Ground
Opening Times: Daily 9.30am to 5.30pm
Telephone Nº: (01204) 389200
Postal Sales: Yes
Nearest Police Stat'n: Howell Croft, Bolton
Police Telephone Nº: (01204) 522466

GROUND INFORMATION

Away Supporters' Entrances & Sections:
Embankment turnstiles for the Embankment – mainly open but a small number of covered seats

ADMISSION INFO (1996/97 PRICES)

Adult Standing: £11.00
Adult Seating: £15.00
Child Standing: £8.00
Child Seating: £9.00
Programme Price: £1.50

DISABLED INFORMATION

Wheelchairs: 4 spaces each for Home and Away fans in the disabled area, Manchester Road Paddock
Helpers: One helper admitted per disabled fan
Prices: Free for disabled fans. Helpers normal prices
Disabled Toilets: Available in the disabled area
Are Bookings Necessary: No
Contact: (01204) 389200

Travelling Supporters' Information:
Routes: From North: Exit M61 at Junction 5 or use A666 or A676. Follow signs for Farnworth (B653) into Manchester Road. After ½ mile turn left into Croft Lane; From South, East and West: Exit M62 at Junction 14 to M61. After 2 miles, leave the motorway then take the 1st exit at the roundabout onto the B6536. After 2 miles, turn right into Croft Lane.

AFC BOURNEMOUTH

Founded: 1890 (**Entered League:** 1923)
Former Names: Boscombe St. Johns FC
(1890-1899); Boscombe FC (1899-1923);
Bournemouth & Boscombe Athletic FC
(1923-1972)
Nickname: 'Cherries'
Ground: Dean Court, Bournemouth,
Dorset   BH7 7AF

Record Attendance: 28,799 (2/3/57)
Colours: Shirts – Red & Black Stripes
    Shorts – White
Telephone Nº: (01202) 395381
Ticket Office: (01202) 395381
Fax Number: (01202) 309797
Pitch Size: 112 × 75 yards
Ground Capacity: 11,000
Seating Capacity: 3,080

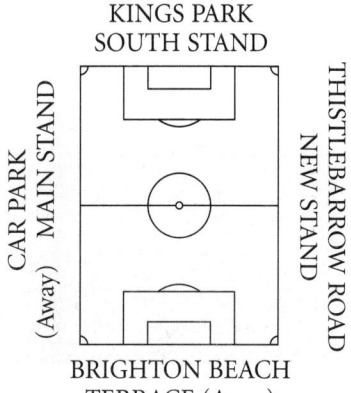

KINGS PARK
SOUTH STAND

CAR PARK (Away)   MAIN STAND

THISTLEBARROW ROAD   NEW STAND

BRIGHTON BEACH
TERRACE (Away)

GENERAL INFORMATION

Supporters Club: c/o Dean Court Supporters' Club,
Bournemouth   BH7 7AF
Telephone Nº: (01202) 398313
Car Parking: Car Park for 1,500 cars behind Main
Stand
Coach Parking: Kings Park (nearby)
Nearest Railway Station: Bournemouth Central
(1½ ml)
Nearest Bus Station: Holdenhurst Road, Bourne-
mouth
Club Shop: At Ground
Opening Times: Weekdays 9.00-5.00; Saturday
Matchdays 1.00pm to kick-off
Telephone Nº: (01202) 397777/395381
Postal Sales: Yes
Nearest Police Stat'n: Boscombe (400 yards)
Police Telephone Nº: (01202) 552099

GROUND INFORMATION

Away Supporters' Entrances & Sections:
Main Stand Turnstiles (Block A) for Brighton Beach
Terrace (open)

ADMISSION INFO (1996/97 PRICES)

Adult Standing: £7.50
Adult Seating: £8.50 – £11.50
Child Standing: £4.00
Child Seating: £4.50 – £6.50
Programme Price: £1.40

DISABLED INFORMATION

Wheelchairs: 16 spaces in total for Home and Away
fans in the disabled section, South Stand
Helpers: One helper admitted per disabled fan
Prices: Free of charge for Disabled and Helpers
Disabled Toilets: Available adjacent to South Stand
Are Bookings Necessary: Yes
Contact: (01202) 395381

Travelling Supporters' Information:
Routes: From North & East: Take A338 into Bournemouth and turn left at 'Kings Park' turning. Then first left at
mini-roundabout and first right into Thistlebarrow Road for ground; From West: Use A3049, turning right at
Wallisdown Roundabout to Talbot Roundabout. Take first exit at Talbot Roundabout (over Wessex Way), then
left at mini-roundabout. Go straight on at traffic lights then right at mini-roundabout into Kings Park for ground.

BRADFORD CITY FC

Founded: 1903 (**Entered League:** 1903)
Former Names: None
Nickname: 'Bantams'
Ground: The Pulse Stadium, Valley Parade, Bradford   BD8 7DY
Record Attendance: 39,146 (11/3/11)
Pitch Size: 110 × 80 yards

Colours: Shirts – Claret & Amber
         Shorts – Black
Telephone Nº: (01274) 773355
Ticket Office: (01274) 773355
Fax Number: (01274) 773356
Ground Capacity: 18,000
Seating Capacity: 11,500 (When new stand completed)

DIAMOND SEAL KOP

N & P STAND

UNDER CONSTRUCTION   NEW STAND

H.S.G. STAND

GENERAL INFORMATION

Supporters Club: c/o Mrs J. Calvert, 1 Westmoor Avenue, Baildon   BD17 5HG
Telephone Nº: (01274) 591947
Car Parking: Street Parking and Car Parks (£2.50 entry charge)
Coach Parking: By Police direction
Nearest Railway Station: Bradford Interchange
Nearest Bus Station: Bradford Interchange (1 mile)
Club Shop: At Ground
Opening Times: Monday to Saturday 9.00-5.00
Telephone Nº: (01274) 773355
Postal Sales: Yes
Nearest Police Station: Tyrrells, Bradford
Police Telephone Nº: (01274) 723422

GROUND INFORMATION

Away Supporters' Entrances & Sections:
H.S.G. Stand

ADMISSION INFO (1996/97 PRICES)

Adult Standing: £9.00
Adult Seating: £13.00
Child Standing: £3.00 (members) – £5.50
Child Seating: £7.50
Programme Price: £1.50

DISABLED INFORMATION

Wheelchairs: 40 spaces in total for Home and Away fans in the disabled area, 'A' Block of the N & P Stand
Helpers: One helper admitted per disabled fan
Prices: Half-price for disabled fans and helpers
Disabled Toilets: Available behind the disabled area
Are Bookings Necessary: Yes
Contact: (01274) 773355

Travelling Supporters' Information:
Routes: From North: Take A650 and follow signs for Bradford. A third of a mile after the junction with the Ring Road turn left into Valley Parade; From East, South and West: Exit M62 at Junction 26 onto M606. At the end take 2nd left from roundabout onto A6177 Ring Road. At the second roundabout turn right onto the Central Ring Road (A6181) then left at the next roundabout and left again following roundabout marked 'Local Access Only'. Pass through traffic lights at the top of the hill following Keighley (A650) sign. Ground is ½ mile on right.

BRENTFORD FC

Founded: 1889 (**Entered League:** 1920)
Former Names: None
Nickname: 'Bees'
Ground: Griffin Park, Braemar Road, Brentford, Middlesex   TW8 0NT
Record Attendance: 39,626 (5/3/38)
Pitch Size: 111 × 74 yards

Colours: Shirts – Red and White Stripes
        Shorts – Black
Telephone Nº: (0181) 847-2511
Ticket Office: (0181) 847-2511
Fax Number: (0181) 568-9940
Ground Capacity: 12,951
Seating Capacity: 9,108

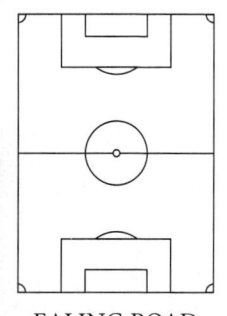

SEATS & TERRACING
BROOK ROAD

BRAEMAR ROAD
MAIN STAND

NEW ROAD
TERRACING

EALING ROAD
TERRACING

GENERAL INFORMATION

Supporters Club: c/o Mr P. Gilham, 16 Hartland Road, Hampton Hill, Middlesex
Telephone Nº: (0181) 941-0425
Car Parking: Street Parking
Coach Parking: Leyton Road Car Park
Nearest Railway Stat'n: Brentford Central (½ mile)
Nearest Tube Station: South Ealing (Piccadilly) (1 mile)
Club Shop: At Ground
Opening Times: Monday to Friday 10.00-5.00 and also Matchdays
Telephone Nº: (0181) 560-9836
Postal Sales: Yes
Nearest Police Stat'n: Brentford
Police Telephone Nº: (0181) 569-9728

GROUND INFORMATION

Away Supporters' Entrances & Sections:
Brook Road

ADMISSION INFO (1996/97 PRICES)

Adult Standing: £8.00
Adult Seating: £9.00 – £14.00
Child Standing: £5.00
Child Seating: £6.00 – £11.00
Programme Price: £1.50

DISABLED INFORMATION

Wheelchairs: 30 spaces in total for Home and Away fans in the disabled section, Braemar Road
Helpers: One helper admitted per disabled fan
Prices: Free of charge for Disabled and Helpers
Disabled Toilets: Available in the disabled section
Commentaries are available for the blind
Are Bookings Necessary: Yes
Contact: (0181) 560-6062

Travelling Supporters' Information:
Routes: From North: Take the A406 North Circular (from the M1/A1) to the Chiswick Roundabout and then along the Great West Road and turn right at the third set of traffic lights into Ealing Road; From East: Take the A406 to the Chiswick Roundabout, then as North; From West: Exit M4 at Junction 2 – down to the Chiswick Roundabout, then as North; From South: Use the A3, M3, A240 or A316 to Kew Road, continue along over Kew Bridge, turn left at the traffic lights, then right at the next traffic lights into Ealing Road.

BRIGHTON & HOVE ALBION FC

Founded: 1900 (**Entered League:** 1920)
Former Names: Brighton & Hove
Rangers FC (1900-1901)
Nickname: 'Seagulls'
Ground: Goldstone Ground, Newtown
Road, Hove, Sussex   BN3 7DE
Record Attendance: 36,747 (27/12/58)

Colours: Shirts – Blue and White Stripes
Shorts – Blue
Telephone Nº: (01273) 778855
Ticket Office: (01273) 778855
Fax Number: (01273) 321095
Pitch Size: 112 × 75 yards
Ground Capacity: 13,600
Seating Capacity: 5,110

OLD SHOREHAM ROAD
NORTH TERRACE

SOUTH STAND
NEWTOWN ROAD

GENERAL INFORMATION
Supporters Club: c/o Liz Costa, 72 Stoneham Road,
Hove   BN3 5HH
Telephone Nº: (01273) 778855
Car Parking: Greyhound Stadium & street parking
Coach Parking: Conway Street, Hove
Nearest Railway Station: Hove (5 minutes walk)
Nearest Bus Station: Brighton Pool Valley
Club Shop: The Albion Shop, Newtown Road
Opening Times: Weekdays 10.00am to 4.00pm
Telephone Nº: (01273) 778855
Postal Sales: Yes
Nearest Police Station: Hove (1 mile)
Police Telephone Nº: (01273) 778922

GROUND INFORMATION
Away Supporters' Entrances & Sections:
Goldstone Lane Turnstiles 5, 6, 7, 8, 9, 10, 46, 47 for
South East Corner (Open) and South Stand (Seats)

ADMISSION INFO (1996/97 PRICES)
Adult Standing: £8.00
Adult Seating: West Stand £12; South Stand £10
Child Standing: £4.00
Child Seating: West Stand £6.00; South Stand £5.00
Programme Price: £1.50

DISABLED INFORMATION
Wheelchairs: 20 spaces in total for Home and Away
fans in the disabled area, S.W. Corner of the ground
Helpers: One helper admitted per disabled fan
Prices: Free of charge for disabled. Helpers £8.00
Disabled Toilets: One available in the disabled area
Are Bookings Necessary: Yes
Contact: (01273) 778855

Travelling Supporters' Information:
Routes: From North: Take A23, then turn right 2 miles after Pyecombe. Follow the Hove signs for 1 mile, bear
left into Nevill Road (A2023). After 1 mile turn left at the crossroads into Old Shoreham Road;   From East: Take
A27 to Brighton and follow the Worthing signs into Old Shoreham Road;   From West: Take A27 straight into
Old Shoreham Road.
Bus Services: Service 11 passes the ground.

BRISTOL CITY FC

Founded: 1894 (**Entered League**: 1901)	**Colours**: Shirts – Red
Former Names: Bristol South End FC	Shorts – White
(1894-1897)	**Telephone Nº**: (0117) 963-2812
Nickname: 'Robins'	**Ticket Office**: (0117) 963-2812
Ground: Ashton Gate, Winterstoke Road,	**Fax Number**: (0117) 963-9574
Ashton Road, Bristol BS3 2EJ	**Pitch Size**: 115 × 75 yards
Record Attendance: 43,335 (16/2/35)	**Ground Capacity**: 17,888 (All seats)

CARLING ATYEO STAND

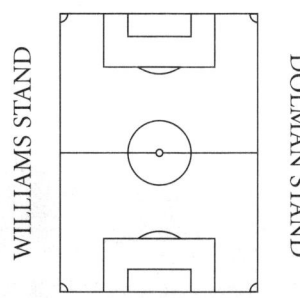

WINTERSTOKE ROAD END
(Covered End) (Away)
(CAR PARK)

GENERAL INFORMATION

Supporters Club: Mr G. Williams, c/o Club
Telephone Nº: (0117) 966-5554
Car Parking: Street Parking
Coach Parking: Winterstoke Road
Nearest Railway Station: Bristol Temple Meads (1½ miles)
Nearest Bus Station: Bristol City Centre
Club Shop: At Ground
Opening Times: Weekdays 10.00am to 6.00pm and Saturdays 9.30am – 12.30am
Telephone Nº: (0117) 953-8566
Postal Sales: Yes
Nearest Police Stat'n: Kings Mead Lane (2 miles) – Office at ground
Police Telephone Nº: (0117) 927-7777

GROUND INFORMATION

Away Supporters' Entrances & Sections:
Winterstoke Road

ADMISSION INFO (1996/97 PRICES)

Adult Seating: £9.00 – £17.00
Child Seating: £4.00 – £16.00
Programme Price: £1.30

DISABLED INFORMATION

Wheelchairs: Limited number accommodated at Pitchside – please apply early
Helpers: One helper admitted per disabled fan
Prices: Free for the disabled. Helpers normal price
Disabled Toilets: 2 available
Commentaries are available for the blind (contact the club for further information)
Are Bookings Necessary: Yes
Contact: (0117) 963-2812

Travelling Supporters' Information:
Routes: From North & West: Exit M5 at Junction 16, take the A38 to Bristol City Centre and follow the A38 Taunton signs. Cross the swing bridge after 1¼ miles and bear left into Winterstoke Road; From East: Take M4 then M32 and follow signs for the City Centre. Then as for North and West; From South: Exit M5 at Junction 18 and follow Taunton signs over the swing bridge (then as above).
Bus Services: Services 27A and 28A from the Railway Station.

BRISTOL ROVERS FC

Founded: 1883 (**Entered League**: 1920)
Former Names: Black Arabs FC (1883-4);
Eastville Rovers FC (1884-96); Bristol
Eastville Rovers FC (1896-97)
Nickname: 'Pirates'; 'Rovers'
Ground: Memorial Ground, Filton
Avenue, Bristol
Office: The Beeches, Brislington, Bristol,
BS4 5RG

Record Attendance: 18,000
Colours: Shirts – Blue & White Quarters
   Shorts – White
Telephone Nº: (0117) 986-9999
Ticket Office: (0117) 986-9999
Fax Number: (0117) 971-1968
Pitch Size: 115 × 76 yards
Ground Capacity: Approx. 12,000 (When
Seating Capacity: 1,780 work completed)

FILTON AVENUE
CLUB HOUSE TERRACE

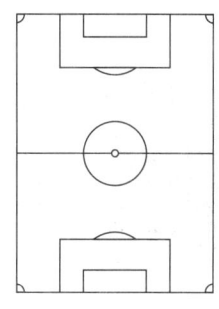

GENERAL INFORMATION
Supporters Club: c/o Mr. Steve Burns, 199 Two
Mile Hill Road, Kingswood   BS15 1AZ
Telephone Nº: (0117) 961-1772
Car Parking: Approximately 300 spaces at ground
(pre-booked) and street parking
Coach Parking: At the ground
Nearest Railway Station: Temple Meads (2 miles)
Nearest Bus Station: Bristol City Centre
Club Shop:
Opening Times: Weekdays 9.00am – 5.00pm
Telephone Nº: (0117) 961-1772
Postal Sales: Yes
Nearest Police Station: Bridewell (2 miles)
Police Telephone Nº: (0117) 927-7777

GROUND INFORMATION
Away Supporters' Entrances & Sections:
Centenary Stand, Muller Road

ADMISSION INFO (1996/97 PRICES)
Adult Standing: £8.00
Adult Seating: £13.00
Child Standing: £4.00
Child Seating: No concessions
Programme Price: £1.30

DISABLED INFORMATION
Wheelchairs: Unspecified number accommodated
in front of the Centenary Stand and West Stand
Helpers: One helper admitted per disabled person
Prices: Free of charge for the disabled and helpers
Disabled Toilets: One available in the Centenary
Stand
Are Bookings Necessary: Yes
Contact: (0117) 951-4448

Travelling Supporters' Information:
Routes: From All Parts: Exit M32 at Junction 2 then take 3rd exit at the roundabout (signposted Horfield) into
Muller Road. Continue for approximately 1½ miles passing straight across 3 sets of traffic lights. At the 4th set of
traffic lights turn left into Filton Avenue and the ground is immediately on the left.

BURNLEY FC

Founded: 1882 (**Entered League:** 1888)
Former Names: Burnley Rovers FC
Nickname: 'Clarets'
Ground: Turf Moor, Brunshaw Road,
Burnley, Lancashire BB10 4BX
Record Attendance: 54,775 (23/2/24)

Colours: Shirts – Claret & Blue Quarters
Shorts – White
Telephone N°: (01282) 700000
Ticket Office: (01282) 700010
Fax Number: (01282) 428938
Pitch Size: 114 × 72 yards
Ground Capacity: 22,000 (All seats)

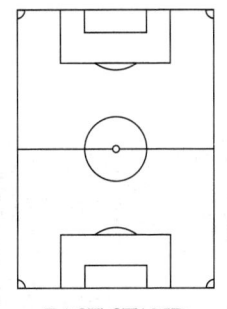

BELVEDERE ROAD
ENDSLEIGH STAND

BRUNSHAW ROAD
BOB LORD STAND

NORTH STAND

EAST STAND

GENERAL INFORMATION

Supporters Club: David Spencer, c/o Club
Telephone N°: (01282) 435176
Car Parking: Ormerod Road, adjacent to the Fire
Station (2 minutes walk) and Fulledge Recreation
Ground (2 minutes walk)
Coach Parking: By Police direction
Nearest Railway Stat'n: Burnley Central (1½ miles)
Nearest Bus Station: Burnley (5 minutes walk)
Club Shop: At Ground
Opening Times: 9.15-5.00 Mondays to Saturday
Matchdays; Friday Evenings 5.00-7.00pm; Saturdays
(no match) 9.15am – 1.00pm
Telephone N°: (01282) 700016
Postal Sales: Yes
Nearest Police Station: Parker Lane, Burnley
(5 minutes walk)
Police Telephone N°: (01282) 425001

GROUND INFORMATION

Away Supporters' Entrances & Sections:
Endsleigh Stand

ADMISSION INFO (1996/97 PRICES)

Adult Seating: £9.00 – £14.00
Child Seating: £4.50 – £7.00
Programme Price: £1.50

DISABLED INFORMATION

Wheelchairs: Limited number of spaces in front of
Bob Lord Stand
Helpers: One helper admitted per disabled fan
Prices: Free for disabled. Concessionary for helpers
Disabled Toilets: None
Commentaries are available via headsets
Are Bookings Necessary: Yes
Contact: (01282) 700000 (Mrs P. Scott)

Travelling Supporters' Information:
Routes: From North: Follow A682 to Town Centre and take first exit at roundabout (Ritzy Nightclub) into
Yorkshire Street. Follow through traffic signals into Brunshaw Road; From East: Follow A646 to A671 then
along Todmorden Road towards Town Centre. At traffic signals (crossroads) turn right into Brunshaw Road; From
West & South: Exit M6 at Junction 31 and take A59 and the A677 towards Blackburn. Then follow A6119 (Blackburn Ring Road) to M65. Exit M65 at Junction 10 and follow signs for Town Centre. At roundabout in centre take
the third exit into Yorkshire Street. Then as North.

BURY FC

Founded: 1885 (**Entered League:** 1894)
Former Names: None
Nickname: 'Shakers'
Ground: Gigg Lane, Bury, Lancashire
BL9 9HR
Record Attendance: 35,000 (9/1/60)
Pitch Size: 112 × 72 yards

Colours: Shirts – White
Shorts – Royal Blue
Telephone Nº: (0161) 764-7674
Ticket Office: (0161) 764-4881
Fax Number: (0161) 764-5521/763-3103
Ground Capacity: 11,200
Seating Capacity: 8,700

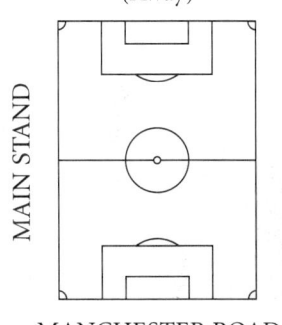

CEMETERY ROAD STAND
(Away)

MAIN STAND

SOUTH STAND

MANCHESTER ROAD
STAND

GENERAL INFORMATION
Supporters Club: P. Cullen, c/o Club
Telephone Nº: –
Car Parking: Street Parking
Coach Parking: By Police direction
Nearest Railway Station: Bury Interchange (1 mile)
Nearest Bus Station: Bury Interchange
Club Shop: At Ground
Opening Times: Daily 9.00am to 5.00pm
Telephone Nº: (0161) 705-2144
Postal Sales: Yes (Price lists available)
Nearest Police Station: Irwell Street, Bury
Police Telephone Nº: (0161) 872-5050

GROUND INFORMATION
Away Supporters' Entrances & Sections:
Gigg Lane entrance for the Cemetery Road Stand
(May be subject to change)

ADMISSION INFO (1996/97 PRICES)
Adult Standing: £8.00
Adult Seating: £10.00 – £12.00
Child Standing: £8.00
Child Seating: £5.00 – £6.00
Programme Price: £1.50

DISABLED INFORMATION
Wheelchairs: Accommodation not specified
Helpers: Admitted – number not specified
Prices: Disabled half-price. Helpers normal price
Disabled Toilets: Available in disabled section
A Radio Commentary is available in the Press Box
Are Bookings Necessary: Yes
Contact: (0161) 764-4881

Travelling Supporters' Information:
Routes: From North: Exit M66 at Junction 2, take Bury Road (A58) for ½ mile, then turn left into Heywood Street and follow this into Parkhills Road until its end, turn left into Manchester Road (A56) and then left again into Gigg Lane. From South, East & West: Exit M62 at Junction 17, take Bury Road (A56) for 3 miles and then turn right into Gigg Lane.

CAMBRIDGE UNITED FC

Founded: 1919 (**Entered League:** 1970)
Former Names: Abbey Utd FC (1919-49)
Nickname: 'U's'; 'United'
Ground: Abbey Stadium, Newmarket Road, Cambridge   CB5 8LN
Record Attendance: 14,000 (1/5/70)
Pitch Size: 110 × 74 yards

Colours: Shirts – Amber
Shorts – Black
Telephone Nº: (01223) 566500
Ticket Office: (01223) 566500
Fax Number: (01223) 566502
Ground Capacity: 9,667
Seating Capacity: 3,265

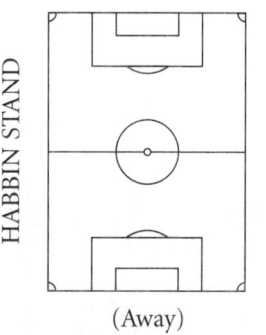

NEWMARKET ROAD
NORTH TERRACE

HABBIN STAND

Disabled

MAIN STAND

(Away)
SOUTH TERRACE

GENERAL INFORMATION

Supporters Club: c/o Club
Telephone Nº: –
Car Parking: Coldhams Common (No street parking)
Coach Parking: Coldhams Common
Nearest Railway Station: Cambridge (2 miles)
Nearest Bus Station: Cambridge City Centre
Club Shop: At Ground
Opening Times: Weekdays & Matchdays 10.00-5.00
Telephone Nº: (01223) 566503
Postal Sales: Yes
Nearest Police Station: Parkside, Cambridge
Police Telephone Nº: (01223) 358966

GROUND INFORMATION

Away Supporters' Entrances & Sections:
Coldham Common turnstiles 20-23 – South Terrace

ADMISSION INFO (1996/97 PRICES)

Adult Standing: £7.00
Adult Seating: £7.00 – £12.00
Child Standing: £4.00
Child Seating: £4.00 – £6.00
Programme Price: £1.50

DISABLED INFORMATION

Wheelchairs: 12 spaces in total for Home and Away fans in the disabled section, in front of Main Stand
Helpers: One helper admitted per disabled fan
Prices: Free for the disabled. £7.00 for helpers
Disabled Toilets: Available at the rear of the disabled enclosure
Are Bookings Necessary: Yes
Contact: (01223) 566500

Travelling Supporters' Information:
Routes: From North: Take A1 and A604 into the City Centre, then take the A45. Turn off onto the B1047, signposted for Cambridge Airport, Horningsea and Fen Ditton. Turn right at the top of the slip road and travel through Fen Ditton. Turn right at the traffic lights at the end of the village. Go straight on at the roundabout onto Newmarket Road. The ground is 500 yards on the left; From South & East: Take A10 or A130 into Cambridge and join A45. Then as North; From West: Take A 422 to Cambridge and join the A45. Then as North.
Bus Services: Services 180 & 181 from Railway Station to City Centre. 182 & 183 to the Ground.

CARDIFF CITY FC

Founded: 1899 (**Entered League:** 1920)
Former Names: Riverside FC (1899-1910)
Nickname: 'Bluebirds'
Ground: Ninian Park, Sloper Road,
Cardiff   CF1 8SX
Record Attendance: 61,566 (14/10/61)
Pitch Size: 112 × 76 yards

Colours: Shirts – Blue
    Shorts – Blue
Telephone Nº: (01222) 398636
Ticket Office: (01222) 398636
Fax Number: (01222) 341148
Ground Capacity: 13,695
Seating Capacity: 11,371

GRANGETOWN END
(Away)

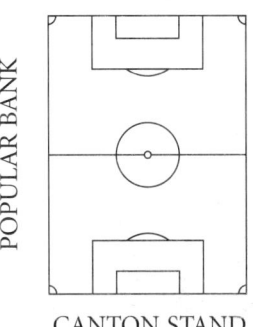

CANTON STAND

GENERAL INFORMATION

Supporters Club: Jackie Rockey, c/o Club
Telephone Nº: –
Car Parking: Sloper Road & Street Parking
Coach Parking: Sloper Road (adjacent)
Nearest Railway Station: Cardiff Central (1 mile)
Nearest Bus Station: Cardiff Central
Club Shop: At Ground
Opening Times: Weekdays 9.00am – 5.00pm and
Matchdays 1½ hours before kick-off
Telephone Nº: (01222) 398636
Postal Sales: Yes
Nearest Police Station: Cowbridge Road East,
Cardiff (1 mile)
Police Telephone Nº: (01222) 222111

GROUND INFORMATION

Away Supporters' Entrances & Sections:
Grangetown End, Sloper Road for 'A' Block
Grandstand and Grangetown End (Open)

ADMISSION INFO (1996/97 PRICES)

Adult Standing: £8.00
Adult Seating: £10.00 – £12.00
Child Standing: £4.00
Child Seating: £5.00 – £6.00
Programme Price: £1.50

DISABLED INFORMATION

Wheelchairs: 20 spaces each for Home and Away
fans in the disabled section, in the Canton Stand/
Popular Bank Corner
Helpers: One helper admitted per disabled fan
Prices: Disabled free of charge. Helpers £8.00
Disabled Toilets: None
Are Bookings Necessary: No
Contact: (01222) 398636

Travelling Supporters' Information:
Routes: From All Parts: Exit M4 at Junction 33 and follow Penarth (A4232) signs. After 6 miles, take the B4267
to Ninian Park.

CARLISLE UNITED FC

Founded: 1903 (**Entered League:** 1928) **Former Names:** Amalgamation of Shaddongate United FC & Carlisle Red Rose FC **Nickname:** 'Cumbrians'; 'Blues' **Ground:** Brunton Park Stadium, Warwick Road, Carlisle CA1 1LL **Record Attendance:** 27,500 (5/1/57)	**Colours:** Shirts – Royal Blue Shorts – White **Telephone Nº:** (01228) 26237 **Ticket Office:** (01228) 26237 **Fax Number:** (01228) 30138 **Pitch Size:** 117 × 78 yards **Ground Capacity:** 16,651 **Seating Capacity:** 8,036

WARWICK ROAD END

EAST STAND   MAIN STAND PADDOCK

PETTERIL END

GENERAL INFORMATION

Supporters Club: M. Hudson, c/o Club
Telephone Nº: (01228) 24014
Car Parking: Rear of Ground via St. Aidans Road
Coach Parking: St. Aidans Road Car Park
Nearest Railway Station: Carlisle Citadel (1 mile)
Nearest Bus Station: Lowther Street, Carlisle
Club Shop: At Ground
Opening Times: Weekdays 9.00am – 5.00pm
Saturday Matchdays 10.00am – 3.00pm
Telephone Nº: (01228) 24014
Postal Sales: Yes
Nearest Police Station: Rickergate, Carlisle (1½ mls)
Police Telephone Nº: (01228) 28191

GROUND INFORMATION

Away Supporters' Entrances & Sections:
Turnstiles 22 to 25

ADMISSION INFO (1996/97 PRICES)

Adult Standing: £7.50
Adult Seating: £9.50 or £11.00
Child Standing: £4.50
Child Seating: £5.50 (in Family Stand)
Programme Price: £1.50

DISABLED INFORMATION

Wheelchairs: Limited number of spaces in the disabled section, in front of the Paddock
Helpers: One helper admitted per disabled fan
Prices: Will advise when booking
Disabled Toilets: None
Commentaries are available for the blind
Are Bookings Necessary: Yes
Contact: (01228) 26237

Travelling Supporters' Information:
Routes: From North, South & East: Exit M6 at Junction 43 and follow signs for Carlisle (A69) into Warwick Road; From West: Take A69 straight into Warwick Road.

CHARLTON ATHLETIC FC

Founded: 1905 (**Entered League:** 1921)
Former Names: None
Nickname: 'Addicks'
Ground: The Valley, Floyd Road,
Charlton, London SE7 8BL
Record Attendance: 75,031 (12/2/38)
Pitch Size: 111 × 73 yards

Colours: Shirts – Red
Shorts – White
Telephone Nº: (0181) 293-4567
Ticket Office: (0181) 858-5888
Fax Number: (0181) 293-5143 (General
Office); (0181) 853-4001 (Box Office)
Ground Capacity: 15,000 (All seats)

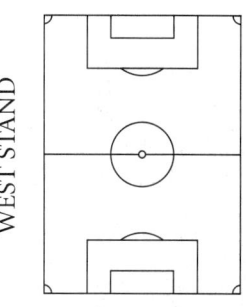

HARVEY GARDENS
NORTH STAND

WEST STAND

EAST STAND

(Away)
SOUTH STAND
VALLEY GROVE

GENERAL INFORMATION
Supporters Club: Craig Norris, P.O. Box 387,
London SE9 6EH
Telephone Nº: (0181) 304-1593
Car Parking: Street Parking
Coach Parking: By Police direction
Nearest Railway Station: Charlton (2 minutes walk)
Nearest Bus Station: –
Club Shop: At Ground
Opening Times: Weekdays 10.00am – 6.00pm
Saturdays 10.00am – 2.45pm
Telephone Nº: (0181) 293-4567
Postal Sales: Yes
Nearest Police Station: Greenwich (2 miles)
Police Telephone Nº: (0181) 853-8212

GROUND INFORMATION
Away Supporters' Entrances & Sections:
Valley Grove South

ADMISSION INFO (1996/97 PRICES)
Adult Seating: £8.00 or £13.00 Members
£13.00 or £15.00 Non-members
Child Seating: £4.00 – £9.00
(Junior Reds £1.00 in Family Area)
Programme Price: £1.50

DISABLED INFORMATION
Wheelchairs: 40 spaces in total for Home and Away
fans in the disabled areas, West Stand and East Stand
Helpers: Up to 40 helpers admitted
Prices: Free of charge for disabled fans and helpers
Disabled Toilets: Available in West and East Stands
Commentaries are available – please ring for details
Are Bookings Necessary: Yes
Contact: (0181) 858-5888

Travelling Supporters' Information:
Routes: From All Parts: Exit M25 at Junction 2 (A2 London-bound) and follow until the road becomes A102(M).
Take the exit marked Woolwich Ferry and turn right along the A206 Woolwich Road. Turn right at the first set of
traffic lights and Floyd Road is the 2nd turning on the left.

CHELSEA FC

Founded: 1905 **(Entered League:** 1905)
Former Names: None
Nickname: 'Blues'
Ground: Stamford Bridge, Fulham Road, London   SW6 1HS
Record Attendance: 82,905 (12/10/35)
Pitch Size: 114 × 71 yards

Colours: Shirts – Blue
     Shorts – Blue
Telephone Nº: (0171) 385-5545
Ticket Office: (0171) 386-7799
Fax Number: (0171) 381-4831
Ground Capacity: 31,000 (All seats)
Note: Redevelopment is progressing

SOUTH TERRACE

EAST STAND (Away)

WEST STAND

NORTH TERRACE

GENERAL INFORMATION

Supporters Club: Pippa Robinson, c/o Club
Telephone Nº: (0171) 385-5545
Car Parking: Underground car park at ground
Coach Parking: By Police direction
Nearest Railway Stat'n: Fulham Broadway (5 mins.)
Nearest Tube Station: Fulham Broadway (District)
Club Shop: At Ground
Opening Times: Weekdays 9.00am – 5.00pm and Matchdays
Telephone Nº: (0171) 381-4569
Club Shop Fax: (0171) 381-5697
Postal Sales: Yes
Nearest Police Stat'n: Fulham
Police Telephone Nº: (0171) 385-1212

GROUND INFORMATION

Away Supporters' Entrances & Sections:
East Stand

ADMISSION INFO (1995/96 PRICES)

Adult Seating: £10.00 – £35.00   Prices depend on class of game, place where seated, and whether or not you are members. Also special rates in the Family Section. Phone club for further details
Child Seating: £5.00 – £6.00
Programme Price: £2.00

DISABLED INFORMATION

Wheelchairs: 40 spaces in total for Home and Away fans in the disabled area, in front of South Terrace
Helpers: One helper admitted per disabled person
Prices: Free for the disabled. Helpers full price
Disabled Toilets: Available in the East Stand Concourse and also in the North Stand
Are Bookings Necessary: Yes
Contact: (0171) 385-5545

Travelling Supporters' Information:
Routes: From North & East: Follow Central London signs from A1/M1 to Hyde Park Corner, then signs for Guildford (A3) to Knightsbridge (A4). After 1 mile turn left into Fulham Road; From South: Take A13 or A24 then A219 to cross Putney Bridge and follow signs for 'West End' (A304) to join the A308 into Fulham Road; From West: Take M4 then A4 to Central London, then signs to Westminster (A3220). After ¾ mile, turn right at the crossroads into Fulham Road.

CHESTER CITY FC

Founded: 1884 (**Entered League:** 1931)
Former Names: Chester FC
Nickname: 'Blues'; 'City'
Ground: The Deva Stadium, Bumpers Lane, Chester CH1 4LT
Record Attendance: 5,638 (2/4/94)
Pitch Size: 115 × 75 yards

Colours: Shirts – Blue and White Stripes
Shorts – Blue and White
Telephone Nº: (01244) 371376
Ticket Office: (01244) 371376
Fax Number: (01244) 390265
Ground Capacity: 6,000
Seating Capacity: 3,408

SOUTH TERRACE
(Away)

EAST STAND
Jewson Family Area

WEST STAND

NORTH TERRACE

GENERAL INFORMATION

Supporters Club: B. Hipkiss, c/o Club
Telephone Nº: (01244) 371376
Car Parking: Ample at ground
Coach Parking: At ground
Nearest Railway Station: Chester (1½ miles)
Nearest Bus Station: Chester (¾ mile)
Club Shop: At Ground
Opening Times: Weekdays & matchdays 9am – 5pm
Telephone Nº: (01244) 390243
Postal Sales: Yes
Nearest Police Station: Chester (¾ mile)
Police Telephone Nº: (01244) 350222

GROUND INFORMATION

Away Supporters' Entrances & Sections:
South Terrace for covered accommodation

ADMISSION INFO (1996/97 PRICES)

Adult Standing: £7.00
Adult Seating: £9.00 (concessions available
Child Standing: £4.50 in the Family Enclosure)
Child Seating: £6.00
Programme Price: £1.50

DISABLED INFORMATION

Wheelchairs: 72 spaces in total for Home and Away fans in the disabled areas, West Stand and East Stand
Helpers: One helper admitted per disabled person
Prices: Free for the disabled. Helpers normal price
Disabled Toilets: Available in West and East Stands
Are Bookings Necessary: Yes
Contact: (01244) 371376

Travelling Supporters' Information:
Routes: From North: Take the M56, A41 or A56 into the Town Centre and then follow Queensferry (A548) signs into Sealand Road. Turn left at the traffic lights by 'Texas' into Bumpers Lane – the ground is ½ mile at the end of the road; From East: Take A54 or A51 into the Town Centre (then as North); From South: Take A41 or A483 into Town Centre (then as North); From West: Take A55, A494 or A548 and follow Queensferry signs towards Birkenhead (A494) and after 1¼ miles bear left onto the A548 (then as North); From M6/M56 (Avoiding Town Centre): Take M56 to Junction 16 (signposted Queensferry), turn left at the roundabout onto A5117, signposted Wales. At next roundabout turn left onto the A5480 (signposted Chester) and after approximately 3 miles take the 3rd exit from the roundabout (signposted Sealand Road Industrial Parks). Go straight across 2 sets of traffic lights into Bumpers Lane. The ground is ½ mile on the right.

CHESTERFIELD FC

Founded: 1866 (**Entered League:** 1899)
Former Names: Chesterfield Town FC
Nickname: 'Spireites'; 'Blues'
Ground: Recreation Ground, Saltergate, Chesterfield   S40 4SX
Record Attendance: 30,968 (7/4/39)
Pitch Size: 112 × 73 yards

Colours: Shirts – Blue and White
Shorts – White
Telephone Nº: (01246) 209765
Ticket Office: (01246) 209765
Fax Number: (01246) 556799
Ground Capacity: 8,954
Seating Capacity: 2,608

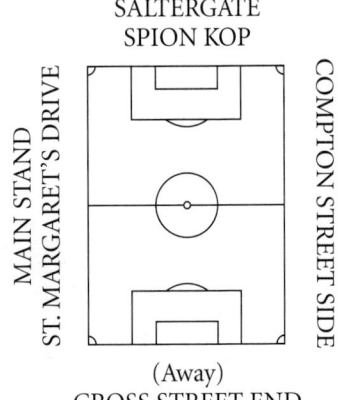

SALTERGATE
SPION KOP

MAIN STAND
ST. MARGARET'S DRIVE

COMPTON STREET SIDE

(Away)
CROSS STREET END

GENERAL INFORMATION

Supporters Club: c/o Club
Telephone Nº: (01246) 209765
Car Parking: Saltergate Car Parks (½ mile)
Coach Parking: By Police direction
Nearest Railway Station: Chesterfield (1 mile)
Nearest Bus Station: Chesterfield
Club Shop: At Ground
Opening Times: Matchdays only
Telephone Nº: (01246) 231535
Postal Sales: Yes
Nearest Police Station: Chesterfield (¾ mile)
Police Telephone Nº: (01246) 220100

GROUND INFORMATION

Away Supporters' Entrances & Sections:
Cross Street turnstiles for Cross Street End (open)

ADMISSION INFO (1996/97 PRICES)

Adult Standing: £8.00
Adult Seating: £9.00 – £10.00
Child Standing: £3.50
Child Seating: £4.00 – £4.50
Home Fans Only – Family Stand Tickets:
1 Adult + 1 Child – £10.00
1 Adult + 2 Children – £11.00
Programme Price: £1.30

DISABLED INFORMATION

Wheelchairs: 20 spaces in total for Home and Away fans below the Saltergate Wing Stand
Helpers: One helper admitted per disabled person
Prices: Free of charge for disabled. Helpers £9.00
Disabled Toilets: One available underneath the Main Stand
Are Bookings Necessary: Yes
Contact: (01246) 209765

Travelling Supporters' Information:
Routes: From North: Exit M1 at Junction 30 then take the A619 into the Town Centre. Follow signs for Old Brampton into Saltergate; From South and East: Take A617 into Town Centre (then as North); From West: Take A619 and when into the Town take the 1st exit at the roundabout into Foljambe Road. Follow to the end of the road, then turn right into Saltergate.

COLCHESTER UNITED FC

Founded: 1937 (**Entered League:** 1950)
Former Names: The Eagles
Nickname: 'U's'
Ground: Layer Road Ground, Colchester, CO2 7JJ
Record Attendance: 19,072 (27/11/48)
Pitch Size: 110 × 70 yards

Colours: Shirts – Royal blue & white stripes
Shorts – White
Telephone N⁰: (01206) 574042
Ticket Office: (01206) 574042
Fax Number: (01206) 48700
Ground Capacity: 7,944
Seating Capacity: 1,150

LAYER ROAD END
(Away)

POPULAR SIDE
FAMILY ENCLOSURE
MAIN STAND

Open Terracing
(FORMERLY CLOCK END)

GENERAL INFORMATION

Supporters Club: Chris Hazlehurst, c/o Club
Telephone N⁰: (01206) 574042
Car Parking: Street Parking
Coach Parking: Boadicea Way (¼ mile)
Nearest Railway Station: Colchester North (2 miles)
Nearest Bus Station: Colchester Town Centre
Club Shop: At ground, + 2nd shop in Town Centre
Opening Times: At ground: Thursdays and Saturdays 9.30am – 4.30pm
Town Centre: Monday to Saturday 9.00am – 5.30pm
Telephone N⁰: (01206) 574042 and 561180
Postal Sales: Yes
Nearest Police Stat'n: Southway, Colchester (½ ml.)
Police Telephone N⁰: (01206) 762212

GROUND INFORMATION

Away Supporters' Entrances & Sections:
Layer Road End turnstiles

ADMISSION INFO (1996/97 PRICES)

Adult Standing: £7.00 (Family Terrace £6.00)
Adult Seating: £7.50 – £9.00 (Family Terrace £9.00)
Child Standing: £5.00 (Family Terrace £3.00)
Child Seating: £5.50 – £6.50 (Family Terrace £5.00)
Programme Price: £1.30

DISABLED INFORMATION

Wheelchairs: 6 spaces in total for Home and Away fans on the Terrace next to the Main Stand
Helpers: One helper admitted per wheelchair
Prices: Free for disabled. Terrace price for helpers
Disabled Toilets: Available under the Main Stand
Commentaries are available for up to 3 people
Are Bookings Necessary: Yes
Contact: (01206) 574042

Travelling Supporters' Information:
Routes: From North: Take A134, B1508 or A12 into the Town Centre then follow signs to Layer (B1026) into Layer Road; From South: Take A12 and follow signs to Layer (B1026) into Layer Road; From West: Take A604 or A120 into the Town Centre then follow signs to Layer (B1026) into Layer Road.

COVENTRY CITY FC

Founded: 1883 (**Entered League**: 1919)	**Colours**: Shirts – Sky Blue / White Trim
Former Names: Singers FC (1883-1898)	Shorts – Sky Blue
Nickname: 'Sky Blues'	**Telephone N°**: (01203) 234000
Ground: Highfield Road Stadium, King	**Ticket Office**: (01203) 234020
Richard Street, Coventry CV2 4FW	**Fax Numbers**: (01203) 234099 (General
Record Attendance: 51,455 (29/4/67)	Office); (01203) 234023 (Ticket Office)
Pitch Size: 110 × 76 yards	**Ground Capacity**: 24,003 (All seats)

SWAN LANE
EAST STAND

KING RICHARD STREET
MAIN STAND

MITCHELLS & BUTLER STAND
(THACKHALL STREET)

CO-OP BANK STAND
NICHOLL STREET
FAMILY STAND

GENERAL INFORMATION

Supporters Club: The Secretary, Coventry City Supporters' Club, Freehold Street, Coventry
Telephone N°: –
Car Parking: Street Parking
Coach Parking: By Police direction
Nearest Railway Station: Coventry (1 mile)
Nearest Bus Station: Coventry (1 mile)
Bus Services to Ground: C16/C35/C36/C37/C7/C8/C24/C26/C27/C31A/C31C/C32/66/778
Club Shop: At Ground
Opening Times: Daily except Sundays (office hours)
Telephone N°: (01203) 234030
Postal Sales: Yes
Nearest Police Station: Little Park Street, Coventry (1 mile)
Police Telephone N°: (01203) 539010

GROUND INFORMATION

Away Supporters' Entrances & Sections:
Thackhall Street for Mitchells & Butler Stand

ADMISSION INFO (1996/97 PRICES)

Adult Seating: £15.00 – £20.00
Child Seating: £7.50 – £10.00
Programme Price: £1.50

DISABLED INFORMATION

Wheelchairs: 24 spaces in total for Home and Away fans in the disabled section in the Clock Stand
Helpers: Up to 47 helpers admitted
Prices: Free for the disabled. Helpers £18.00
Disabled Toilets: 2 are adjacent to the disabled area
Commentaries available via Hospital Radio
Are Bookings Necessary: Yes
Contact: (01203) 234020

Travelling Supporters' Information:
Routes: From North, West & South: Exit M6 at Junction 2. Take A4600 and follow signs for 'City Centre'. Follow this road for aprroximately 3 miles and, just under new road bridge, turn right at traffic lights into Swan Lane; From East: Take M45 then A45 to Ryton-on-Dunsmore. After 1½ miles take the 3rd exit at the roundabout (A423), then after 1¼ miles turn right onto B4110, follow to T-junction and turn left then right into Swan Lane.

CREWE ALEXANDRA FC

Founded: 1877 (**Entered League:** 1892)
Former Names: None
Nickname: 'Railwaymen'
Ground: Gresty Road Ground, Crewe, Cheshire CW2 6EB
Record Attendance: 20,000 (30/1/60)
Pitch Size: 112 × 74 yards

Colours: Shirts – Red
Shorts – White
Telephone Nº: (01270) 213014
Ticket Office: (01270) 252610
Fax Number: (01270) 216320
Ground Capacity: 5,900
Seating Capacity: 4,536

FAMILY STAND

RINGWAY STAND

MAIN STAND

(Away)
GRESTY ROAD END

GENERAL INFORMATION

Supporters Club: c/o Glynn Steele, 18 Gresty Road, Crewe
Telephone Nº: (01270) 255206
Car Parking: Car Park at ground (200 cars)
Coach Parking: Car Park at ground
Nearest Railway Station: Crewe (5 minutes walk)
Nearest Bus Station: Crewe Town
Club Shop: At Ground
Opening Times: Monday to Thursday and Matchdays 9.00am –5.00pm
Telephone Nº: (01270) 213014
Postal Sales: Yes
Nearest Police Station: Crewe Town (1 mile)
Police Telephone Nº: (01270) 500222

GROUND INFORMATION

Away Supporters' Entrances & Sections:
Gresty Road Entrances for Gresty Road seating

ADMISSION INFO (1996/97 PRICES)

Adult Standing: £8.00
Adult Seating: £9.50
Child Standing: £6.00
Child Seating: £7.00 (£5.00 in Family Stand – Junior Red Members only)
Programme Price: £1.30

DISABLED INFORMATION

Wheelchairs: Approximately 7 spaces in total in the disabled areas, Family Stand, Ringway Stand and the Gresty Road End
Helpers: One helper admitted per disabled person
Prices: £5.00 in total for each disabled fan & helper
Disabled Toilets: Available in the Family Stand Commentaries are available for the blind
Are Bookings Necessary: Yes
Contact: (01270) 213014

Travelling Supporters' Information:
Routes: From North: Exit M6 at Junction 17 and take Crewe (A534) road, and at Crewe roundabout follow Chester signs into Nantwich Road. The take a left turn into Gresty Road; From South & East: Take A52 to A5020, then on to Crewe roundabout (then as North); From West: Take A534 into Crewe and turn right just before the railway station into Gresty Road.

CRYSTAL PALACE FC

Founded: 1905 (**Entered League:** 1920)
Former Names: None
Nickname: 'Eagles'
Ground: Selhurst Park, London
SE25 6PU
Record Attendance: 51,482 (11/5/79)
Pitch Size: 110 × 74 yards

Colours: Shirts – Red with Blue Stripes
Shorts – Red
Telephone N°: (0181) 768-6000
Ticket Office: (0181) 771-8841
Fax Number: (0181) 771-5311
Ground Capacity: 26,309 (All seats)

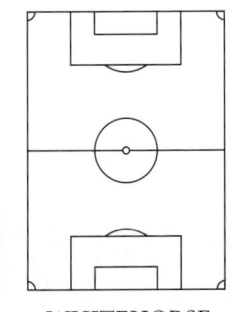

HOLMESDALE ROAD STAND

PARK ROAD — ARTHUR WAIT STAND

CLIFTON ROAD MAIN STAND

WHITEHORSE LANE STAND

GENERAL INFORMATION

Supporters Club: Terry Byfield, c/o Club
Telephone N°: (0181) 768-6020
Car Parking: Street Parking & Sainsbury Car Park near the ground
Coach Parking: Thornton Heath
Nearest Railway Station: Selhurst/Norwood Junction (5 minutes walk)
Nearest Bus Station: Norwood Junction
Club Shop: At Ground
Opening Times: Weekdays & Matchdays 9.30–5.30
Telephone N°: (0181) 653-5584
Postal Sales: Yes
Nearest Police Station: South Norwood (15 mins. walk)
Police Telephone N°: (0181) 653-8568

GROUND INFORMATION

Away Supporters' Entrances & Sections:
Park Road for the Arthur Wait Stand

ADMISSION INFO (1995/96 PRICES)

Adult Seating: £16.00 to £20.00
Child Seating: £12.00 to £15.00
Note: Prices vary depending on the game
Programme Price: £1.50

DISABLED INFORMATION

Wheelchairs: 24 spaces for Home fans; 4 spaces for Away fans in disabled area, Holmesdale Road Stand
Helpers: One helper admitted per wheelchair
Prices: Free for the disabled. Helpers pay full price
Disabled Toilets: Located in the disabled section Commentaries are available for 12 people
Are Bookings Necessary: Yes
Contact: (0181) 768-6000

Travelling Supporters' Information:
Routes: From North: Take M1/A1 to North Circular (A406) to Chiswick. Then take the South Circular (A205) to Wandsworth and then the A3 to the A214 and follow signs to Streatham to the A23. Turn left onto the B273 after 1 mile, follow to the end and turn left into the High Street and into Whitehorse Lane; From East: Take A232 (Croydon Road) to Shirley and join A215 (Northwood Road). After 2¼ miles turn left into Whitehorse Lane; From South: Take A23 and follow signs for Crystal Palace (B266) through Thornton Heath into Whitehorse Lane; From West: Take the M4 to Chiswich (then as North).

DARLINGTON FC

Founded: 1883 (**Entered League:** 1921)
Former Names: None
Nickname: 'Quakers'
Ground: Feethams Ground, Darlington, DL1 5JB
Record Attendance: 21,023 (14/11/60)
Pitch Size: 110 × 74 yards

Colours: Shirts – White and Black
Shorts – Black
Telephone Nº: (01325) 465097
Ticket Office: (01325) 465097
Fax Number: (01325) 381377
Ground Capacity: 7,048
Seating Capacity: 1,105

VICTORIA ROAD
FEETHAMS CRICKET GROUND

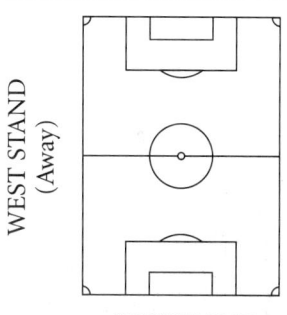

WEST STAND (Away) · EAST STAND BEING REDEVELOPED

SOUTH END
POLAM LANE

GENERAL INFORMATION

Supporters Club: c/o K. Davies, 60 Harrison Terrace, Darlington
Telephone Nº: (01325) 350161
Car Parking: Street Parking
Coach Parking: By Police direction
Nearest Railway Station: Darlington
Nearest Bus Station: Darlington Central
Club Shop: At Ground
Opening Times: Monday – Friday 9.00am – 5.00pm
Telephone Nº: (01325) 465097
Postal Sales: Yes
Nearest Police Station: Park Police Station, Darlington (¼ mile)
Police Telephone Nº: (01325) 467681

GROUND INFORMATION

Away Supporters' Entrances & Sections:
Polam Lane turnstiles for South Terrace (open)

ADMISSION INFO (1996/97 PRICES)

Adult Standing: £7.00
Adult Seating: £8.00 (£7.50 in the Family Stand)
Child Standing: £3.00
Child Seating: £4.00 (£3.50 in the Family Stand)
Programme Price: £1.30

DISABLED INFORMATION

Wheelchairs: 20 spaces in total for Home and Away fans in the disabled section, East Stand
Helpers: One helper admitted per disabled person
Prices: Free of charge for Disabled and Helpers
Disabled Toilets: None
Are Bookings Necessary: Yes
Contact: (01325) 465097

Note: Capacity will change when the new East Stand is complete

Travelling Supporters' Information:
Routes: From North: Take A1(M) to A167 and follow road to the Town Centre, then follow Northallerton signs to Victoria Road; From East: Take A67 to the Town Centre (then as North); From South: Take A1(M) then A66(M) into the Town Centre and then take the 3rd exit at the second roundabout into Victoria Road; From West: Take A67 into the Town Centre and then take the 3rd exit at the roundabout into Victoria Road.

DERBY COUNTY FC

Founded: 1884 **(Entered League:** 1888)
Former Names: None
Nickname: 'Rams'
Ground: Baseball Ground, Shaftesbury
Crescent, Derby   DE23 8NB
Record Attendance: 41,826 (20/9/69)
Pitch Size: 110 × 71 yards

Colours: Shirts – White
   Shorts – Black
Telephone Nº: (01332) 340105
Ticket Office: (01332) 340105
Fax Number: (01332) 293514
Ground Capacity: 17,665 (All seats)

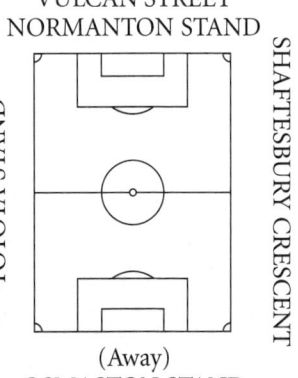

VULCAN STREET
NORMANTON STAND

TOYOTA STAND

SHAFTESBURY CRESCENT

(Away)
OSMASTON STAND

GENERAL INFORMATION

Supporters Club: Mr E. Hallam, c/o Club
Telephone Nº: (01332) 340105
Car Parking: Numerous car parks within ½ mile
Coach Parking: Russell Street
Nearest Railway Station: Derby Midland (1 mile)
and Ramsline Halt (specials only)
Nearest Bus Station: Derby Central
Club Shop: 'Ramtique' at ground
Opening Times: Weekdays 9.30 – 5.00 & Matches
Telephone Nº: (01332) 292081
Postal Sales: Yes
Nearest Police Station: Cotton Lane, Derby
Police Telephone Nº: (01332) 290100

GROUND INFORMATION

Away Supporters' Entrances & Sections:
Turnstiles 48-52 for Osmaston Stand, Lower and
Middle Tiers

ADMISSION INFO (1995/96 PRICES)

Adult Seating: £7.00 – £12.00
Child Seating: £4.00 – £6.00
Programme Price: £1.50

DISABLED INFORMATION

Wheelchairs: 80 spaces in total for Home and Away
fans in the disabled section, Normanton End
Helpers: One helper admitted per disabled person
Prices: Free of charge for Disabled and Helpers
Disabled Toilets: Available in the disabled section
Commentaries are available in the Disabled Viewing
Gallery
Are Bookings Necessary: Yes
Contact: (01332) 340105
Note: It is likely that only season ticket holders will
be admitted during the 1996/97 season.

Travelling Supporters' Information:
Routes: From North: Take A38 into the City Centre then follow signs for Melbourne (A514) and turn right
before the Railway Bridge into Shaftesbury Street; From South, East and West: Take the Derby Ring Road to
Junction with A514 and follow signs to the City Centre into Osmaston Road. After 1¼ miles turn left into
Shaftesbury Street.
Bus Services: Services 159, 188 and 189 pass near the ground. Some special services.

DONCASTER ROVERS FC

Founded: 1879 (**Entered League:** 1901)
Former Names: None
Nickname: 'Rovers'
Ground: Belle Vue, Bawtry Road, Doncaster   DN4 5HT
Record Attendance: 37,149 (2/10/48)
Pitch Size: 110 × 76 yards

Colours: Shirts – Red
Shorts – Red
Telephone Nº: (01302) 539441
Ticket Office: (01302) 539441
Fax Number: (01302) 539679
Ground Capacity: 7,794
Seating Capacity: 1,259

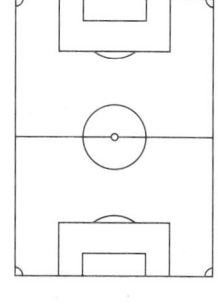

ROSSINGTON END
(Away)

BAWTRY ROAD
MAIN STAND

POPULAR SIDE STAND

GENERAL INFORMATION

Supporters Club: c/o K. Avis, 64 Harrowden Road, Wheatley, Doncaster
Telephone Nº: (01302) 810735
Car Parking: Large car park at ground
Coach Parking: Car park at ground
Nearest Railway Station: Doncaster (1½ miles)
Nearest Bus Station: Doncaster
Club Shop: At Ground
Opening Times: Monday to Friday 1.00 – 4.30pm
Matchdays: 1 hour before and after the game
Telephone Nº: (01302) 535093
Postal Sales: Yes
Nearest Police Station: College Road, Doncaster
Police Telephone Nº: (01302) 366744

GROUND INFORMATION

Away Supporters' Entrances & Sections:
Turnstiles A and 1, 2, 3, 4, 'A' Block for Rossington Road End and 'A' Block of the Main Stand

ADMISSION INFO (1996/97 PRICES)

Adult Standing: £8.00
Adult Seating: £10.00
Child Standing: £4.50 (Under 10's free)
Child Seating: £6.00
Programme Price: £1.50

DISABLED INFORMATION

Wheelchairs: Limited number of spaces available in the disabled section, 'A' Block
Helpers: One helper admitted per wheelchair
Prices: Free of charge for Disabled and Helpers
Disabled Toilets: None
Are Bookings Necessary: Yes
Contact: (01302) 539441

Travelling Supporters' Information:
Routes: From North: Take A1 to A638 into the Town Centre, follow signs for Bawtry (A638) and after 1¼ miles take the 3rd exit at the roundabout into Bawtry Road; From East: Take M18 to A630 and after 2¾ miles take the 1st exit at the roundabout onto A18. After 2½ miles take the first exit at the roundabout into Bawtry Road; From South: Take M1 then M18 to the A6182. After 2 miles take the 3rd exit it the roundabout signposted 'Scunthorpe A18'. Then after 1¼ miles take the 3rd exit at roundabout into Bawtry Road; From West: Take A635 into the Town Centre and follow signs for 'Bawtry' (then as South).

EVERTON FC

Founded: 1878 (**Entered League:** 1888)
Former Names: St. Domingo's FC (1878-1879)
Nickname: 'Blues'; 'Toffeemen'
Ground: Goodison Park, Goodison Road, Liverpool   L4 4EL
Record Attendance: 78,299 (18/9/48)

Colours: Shirts – Blue
  Shorts – White
Telephone Nº: (0151) 330-2200
Ticket Office: (0151) 330-2300
Fax Number: (0151) 523-9666
Pitch Size: 112 × 78 yards
Ground Capacity: 40,000 (All seats)

GOODISON AVENUE
PARK END

BULLENS ROAD

GOODISON ROAD
MAIN STAND

GWLADYS
STREET END

GENERAL INFORMATION

Supporters Club: The Secretary, c/o Club
Telephone Nº: (0151) 330-2208
Car Parking: Corner of Priory Road and Utting Ave.
Coach Parking: Priory Road
Nearest Railway Station: Liverpool Lime Street
Nearest Bus Station: Brownlow Hill, Liverpool
Club Shop: 'Megastore' At Ground
Opening Times: Weekdays and Matchdays 9.00am to 5.00pm and Evening Matches
Telephone Nº: (0151) 330-2333
Postal Sales: Yes – Mail Order and Credit Card Sales
Nearest Police Station: Walton Lane, Liverpool
Police Telephone Nº: (0151) 709-6010

GROUND INFORMATION

Away Supporters' Entrances & Sections:
Bullens Road entrances for Bullens Stand

ADMISSION INFO (1996/97 PRICES)

Adult Seating: £11.00 – £18.00
Child Seating: £6.00   (OAP's £9.00)
Programme Price: £1.50

DISABLED INFORMATION

Wheelchairs: 48 spaces for home fans, 13 spaces for away fans in the disabled section, Bullens Road
Helpers: One helper admitted per wheelchair
Prices: Free for the disabled. Helpers £13.00
Disabled Toilets: Available in the disabled section
Commentaries are available for the blind
Are Bookings Necessary: Yes
Contact: (0151) 330-2300

Travelling Supporters' Information:
Routes: From North: Exit M6 at Junction 24. Take A58 Liverpool Road to A580 and follow into Walton Hall Avenue; From South and East: Exit M6 at Junction 21A onto the M62. At the end of the M62 turn right into Queen's Drive. After 3¾ miles turn left into Walton Hall Avenue; From North Wales: Cross the Mersey into the City Centre and follow signs to Preston (A580) into Walton Hall Avenue.
Bus Services: Services from the City Centre – 19, 20, 21, F1, F9, F2, 30

EXETER CITY FC

Founded: 1904 (**Entered League:** 1920)	**Colours:** Shirts – Red and White Stripes
Former Names: Amalgamation of	Shorts – Black
St. Sidwell United FC & Exeter United FC	**Telephone Nº:** (01392) 54073
Nickname: 'Grecians'	**Ticket Office:** (01392) 54073
Ground: St. James Park, Exeter EX4 6PX	**Fax Number:** (01392) 425885
Record Attendance: 20,984 (4/3/31)	**Ground Capacity:** 10,570
Pitch Size: 114 × 73 yards	**Seating Capacity:** 1,690

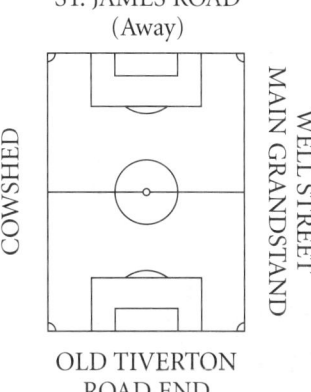

ST. JAMES ROAD
(Away)

COWSHED

MAIN GRANDSTAND

WELL STREET

OLD TIVERTON
ROAD END

GENERAL INFORMATION
Supporters Club: c/o Club
Telephone Nº: (01392) 54073
Car Parking: King William Street
Coach Parking: Paris Street Bus Station
Nearest Railway Station: Exeter St. James Park
(adjacent)
Nearest Bus Station: Paris Street Bus Station
Club Shop: At Ground
Opening Times: Weekdays and Matchdays 9.00am
to 5.00pm
Telephone Nº: (01392) 54073
Postal Sales: Yes
Nearest Police Station: Heavitree Road (½ mile)
Police Telephone Nº: (01392) 52101

GROUND INFORMATION
Away Supporters' Entrances & Sections:
St. James Road turnstiles for St. James Rd. Enclosure

ADMISSION INFO (1996/97 PRICES)
Adult Standing: £7.00
Adult Seating: £9.00
Child Standing: £4.00 (Home Under 16's – £1.00
Child Seating: £6.00 via 'Kid-A-Quid' gates)
Programme Price: £1.50

DISABLED INFORMATION
Wheelchairs: Limited number of spaces available in
front of the Grandstand
Helpers: One helper admitted per wheelchair
Prices: Free of charge for disabled. Helpers £8.00
Disabled Toilets: None
Are Bookings Necessary: Yes
Contact: (01392) 54073

Travelling Supporters' Information:
Routes: From North: Exit M5 at Junction 30 and follow signs to the City Centre along Sidmouth Road and onto
Heavitree Road. Take the 4th exit at the roundabout into Western Way and 2nd exit into Tiverton Road then next
left into St. James Road; From East: Take A30 into Heavitree Road (then as North); From South & West: Take
A38 and follow City Centre signs into Western Way and take the third exit at the roundabout into St. James Road.
Note: This ground is very difficult to find being in a residential area on the side of a hill without prominent
floodlights.

FULHAM FC

Founded: 1879 (**Entered League:** 1907)
Former Names: Fulham St. Andrew's FC
(1879-1898)
Nickname: 'Cottagers'
Ground: Craven Cottage, Stevenage Road,
Fulham, London   SW 6HH
Record Attendance: 49,335 (8/10/38)

Colours: Shirts – White
         Shorts – Black
Telephone Nº: (0171) 736-6561
Ticket Office: (0171) 736-6561
Fax Number: (0171) 731-7047
Pitch Size: 110 × 75 yards
Ground Capacity: 14,969
Seating Capacity: 5,119

PUTNEY END
(Away)

STEVENAGE ROAD STAND
(COTTAGE)

RIVERSIDE STAND

River Thames

HAMMERSMITH END

GENERAL INFORMATION

Supporters Club: Mr M. Tenner, c/o The Club
Telephone Nº: (0171) 736-6561
Car Parking: Street Parking and Henry Compton
School, Kingswood Road
Coach Parking: Stevenage Road
Nearest Railway Station: Putney
Nearest Tube Station: Putney Bridge (District)
Club Shop: At Ground
Opening Times: Home Matchdays, Monday,
Wednesday & Friday afternoons 2.00pm to 4.00pm
Telephone Nº: (0171) 736-6561
Postal Sales: Yes
Nearest Police Station: Heckfield Place, Fulham
Police Telephone Nº: (0171) 385-1212

GROUND INFORMATION

Away Supporters' Entrances & Sections:
Putney End for the Putney Terrace (open)

ADMISSION INFO (1996/97 PRICES)

Adult Standing: £8.00 – £8.50
Adult Seating: £11.50
Child Standing: £4.00 – £4.50
Child Seating: £6.00
Programme Price: £1.50

DISABLED INFORMATION

Wheelchairs: 20 spaces in total for Home and Away
fans, alongside the Miller Stand Touchline
Helpers: One helper admitted per disabled person
Prices: Free of charge for disabled. Helpers £8.00
Disabled Toilets: By forecourt – opposite Cottage
Commentaries are available by prior arrangement
Are Bookings Necessary: Yes
Contact: (0171) 736-6561

Travelling Supporters' Information:
Routes: From North: Take A1/M1 to North Circular (A406) west to Neasden and follow signs for Harlesdon
A404, then Hammersmith A219. At Broadway, follow Fulham sign and turn right after 1 mile into Harboard
Street then left at the end for the ground; From South & East: Take South Circular (A205), follow Putney Bridge
sign (A219). Cross bridge and follow Hammersmith signs for ½ mile, turn left into Bishops Park Road, then right
at the end; From West: Take M4 to A4. Branch left after 2 miles into Hammersmith Broadway (then as North).
Bus Services: Service 74 and 220 from the tube station to the ground.

GILLINGHAM FC

Founded: 1893 (**Entered League:** 1920)	**Colours:** Shirts – Blue
Former Names: New Brompton FC	Shorts – White
(1893-1913)	**Telephone Nº:** (01634) 851854
Nickname: 'Gills'	**Ticket Office:** (01634) 851462
Ground: Priestfield Stadium, Redfern	**Fax Number:** (01634) 850986
Avenue, Gillingham, Kent ME7 4DD	**Ground Capacity:** Approximately 9,000
Pitch Size: 114 × 75 yards	**Seating Capacity:** 3,590 (when the new
Record Attendance: 23,002 (10/1/48)	Gordon Road Stand is complete)

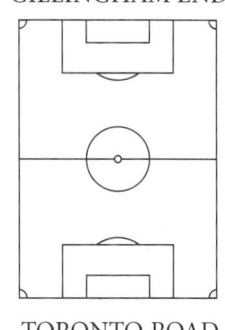

PRIESTFIELD ROAD
GILLINGHAM END

GORDON ROAD STAND
(BEING DEVELOPED)

REDFERN AVENUE
MAINSTAND

TORONTO ROAD
RAINHAM END

GENERAL INFORMATION

Supporters Club: Peter Lloyd, c/o The Club
Telephone Nº: (01634) 851854
Car Parking: Street Parking
Coach Parking: By Police direction
Nearest Railway Station: Gillingham
Nearest Bus Station: Gillingham
Club Shop: At Ground
Opening Times: Weekdays and Matchdays 10.00am
to 5.00pm
Telephone Nº: (01634) 851462
Postal Sales: Yes
Nearest Police Station: Gillingham
Police Telephone Nº: (01634) 234488

GROUND INFORMATION

Away Supporters' Entrances & Sections:
Redfern Avenue turnstiles for Redfern Avenue
Corner (Gillingham End)

ADMISSION INFO (1996/97 PRICES)

Adult Standing: £8.50
Adult Seating: £11.00 – £13.00
Child Standing: £4.00 – £6.50
Child Seating: £7.00 – £13.00
Programme Price: £1.50

DISABLED INFORMATION

Wheelchairs: 20 spaces in total for Home and Away
fans in the disabled section, adjacent to Main Stand
Helpers: One helper admitted per disabled person
Prices: Free for the disabled. Helpers normal prices
Disabled Toilets: None
Are Bookings Necessary: Preferred
Contact: (01634) 851462

Travelling Supporters' Information:
Routes: From All Parts: Exit M2 at Junction 4 and follow the link road (dual carriageway) B278 to the 3rd
roundabout. Turn left onto the A2 (dual carriageway) and go across the roundabout to the traffic lights. Turn
right into Woodlands Road after the traffic lights. The ground is ¼ mile on the left.

GRIMSBY TOWN FC

Founded: 1878 (**Entered League:** 1892)
Former Names: Grimsby Pelham FC
(1879)
Nickname: 'Mariners'
Ground: Blundell Park, Cleethorpes,
DN35 7PY
Record Attendance: 31,651 (20/2/37)

Colours: Shirts – Black and White Stripes
Shorts – Black
Telephone Nº: (01472) 697111
Ticket Office: (01472) 697111
Fax Number: (01472) 693665
Pitch Size: 111 × 74 yards
Ground Capacity: 8,607 (All seats)

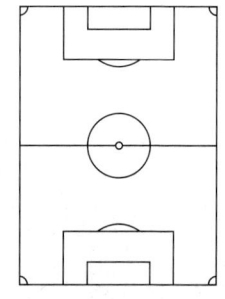

NEVILLE STREET
OSMOND STAND
(Away)

HARRINGTON STREET
MAIN STAND

GRIMSBY ROAD
STONES BITTER STAND

PONTOON STAND
BLUNDELL AVENUE

GENERAL INFORMATION

Supporters Club: c/o Rachel Branson, 26
Humberstone Road, Grimsby
Telephone Nº: (01472) 360050
Car Parking: Street Parking
Coach Parking: Harrington Street – Near Ground
Nearest Railway Station: Cleethorpes (1½ miles)
Nearest Bus Station: Brighowgate, Grimsby (4 mls)
Club Shop: At Ground
Opening Times: Monday – Friday 9.00am – 5.00pm
Match Saturdays 10.00am to kick-off
Telephone Nº: (01472) 697111
Postal Sales: Yes
Nearest Police Station: Cleethorpes (1½ miles)
Police Telephone Nº: (01472) 359171

GROUND INFORMATION

Away Supporters' Entrances & Sections:
Harrington Street turnstiles 15-18 and Constitutional Avenue turnstiles 5-14 for the Osmond Stand

ADMISSION INFO (1996/97 PRICES)

Adult Seating: £10.00 – £12.00 (Away fans £12.00)
Child Seating: £5.00 (No concessions for away fans)
N.B. Special Family rate in the Main Stand
Programme Price: £1.50

DISABLED INFORMATION

Wheelchairs: 50 spaces in total for Home and Away
fans in the disabled section, Main Stand
Helpers: Helpers are admitted
Prices: Free for the disabled. Helpers normal prices
Disabled Toilets: Available in the disabled section
Commentaries are available in the disabled section
Are Bookings Necessary: No
Contact: (01472) 697111

Travelling Supporters' Information:
Routes: From All Parts except Lincolnshire and East Anglia: Take M180 to A180 and follow signs for Grimsby/
Cleethorpes. The A180 ends at a roundabout (the 3rd in short distance after crossing docks), take 2nd exit from
the roundabout over the Railway flyover into Cleethorpes Road (A1098) and continue into Grimsby Road. After
second stretch of dual carriageway, the ground is ½ mile on the left; From Lincolnshire: Take A46 or A16 and
follow Cleethorpes signs along (A1098) Weelsby Road for 2 miles. Take the 1st exit at the roundabout at the end
of Clee Road into Grimsby Road. The ground is 1¾ miles on the right.

HARTLEPOOL UNITED FC

Founded: 1908 (**Entered League:** 1921)
Former Names: Hartlepools United FC
(1908-68); Hartlepool FC (1968-77)
Nickname: 'The Pool'
Ground: Victoria Park, Clarence Road,
Hartlepool   TS24 8BZ
Record Attendance: 17,426 (15/1/57)

Colours: Shirts – Blue and Sky Blue
    Shorts – Blue and Sky Blue
Telephone Nº: (01429) 272584
Ticket Office: (01429) 222077
Fax Number: (01429) 863007
Pitch Size: 113 × 77 yards
Ground Capacity: 7,229
Seating Capacity: 3,966

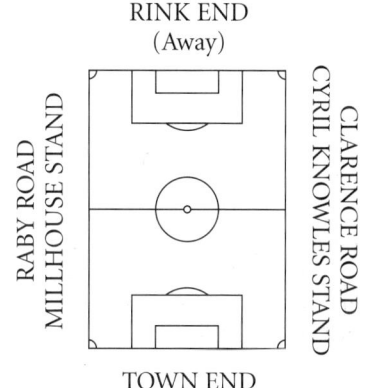

RINK END
(Away)

RABY ROAD
MILLHOUSE STAND

CYRIL KNOWLES STAND
CLARENCE ROAD

TOWN END

GENERAL INFORMATION
Supporters Club: c/o D. Latimer, 4 Friarage
Gardens, Hartlepool
Telephone Nº: –
Car Parking: Street Parking
Coach Parking: Church Street
Nearest Railway Station: Hartlepool Church Street
(5 minutes walk)
Club Shop: At Ground
Opening Times: Weekdays 9.00am – 5.00pm and
Saturdays 9.00am – 2.00pm
Telephone Nº: (01429) 222077
Postal Sales: Yes
Nearest Police Station: Avenue Road, Hartlepool
Police Telephone Nº: (01429) 221151

GROUND INFORMATION
Away Supporters' Entrances & Sections:
Clarence Road turnstiles 1 & 2 for Rink End

ADMISSION INFO (1996/97 PRICES)
Adult Standing: £9.00
Adult Seating: £10.00
Child Standing: £6.00
Child Seating: £7.00
Programme Price: £1.30

DISABLED INFORMATION
Wheelchairs: 20 spaces in total for Home and Away
fans in the disabled section, Cyril Knowles Stand
Helpers: One helper admitted per wheelchair
Prices: Free of charge for Disabled and Helpers
Disabled Toilets: Available in Cyril Knowles Stand
Commentaries are available for the blind
Are Bookings Necessary: No
Contact: (01429) 272584

Travelling Supporters' Information:
Routes: From North: Take A1/A19 then A179 towards Hartlepool to Hart. Straight across traffic lights (2½
miles) to the cross-roads, then turn left into Clarence Road; From South and West: Take A1/A19 or A689 into
Town Centre then turn left into Middleton Road and left again into Clarence Road.

HEREFORD UNITED FC

Founded: 1924 (**Entered League:** 1972)	**Colours:** Shirts – White
Former Names: None	Shorts – Black
Nickname: 'United'; 'The Bulls'	**Telephone Nº:** (01432) 276666
Ground: Edgar Street, Hereford	**Ticket Office:** (01432) 276666
HR4 9JU	**Fax Number:** (01432) 341359
Record Attendance: 18,114 (4/1/58)	**Ground Capacity:** 8,843
Pitch Size: 111 × 74 yards	**Seating Capacity:** 2,761

BLACKFRIARS STREET END
(Away)

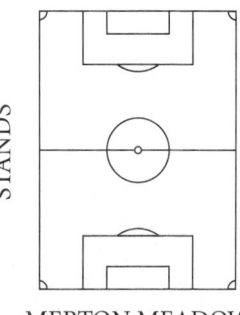

MERTON MEADOW
TERRACES

GENERAL INFORMATION

Supporters Club: K. Benjimen, c/o The Club
Telephone Nº: (01432) 276666
Car Parking: Merton Meadow & Edgar St. car parks
Coach Parking: Cattle Market (Near the ground)
Nearest Railway Station: Hereford (½ mile)
Nearest Bus Station: Commercial Road, Hereford
Club Shop: At Ground
Opening Times: Matchdays and Weekdays via
Commercial Office
Telephone Nº: (01432) 276666
Postal Sales: Yes
Nearest Police Station: Bath Street, Hereford
Police Telephone Nº: (01432) 276422

GROUND INFORMATION

Away Supporters' Entrances & Sections:
Blackfriars Street and Edgar Street for the
Blackfriars Street End

ADMISSION INFO (1996/97 PRICES)

Adult Standing: £6.00 – £7.00
Adult Seating: £8.00 – £9.00
Child Standing: £3.00 – £4.00
Child Seating: £5.00 – £6.00
Programme Price: £1.50

DISABLED INFORMATION

Wheelchairs: 10 spaces in total for Home and Away
fans in the disabled section, Edgar Street side
Helpers: One helper admitted per disabled person
Prices: £6.00 each for both the disabled and helpers
Disabled Toilets: None
Are Bookings Necessary: No
Contact: (01432) 276666

Travelling Supporters' Information:
Routes: From North: Follow A49 Hereford signs straight into Edgar Street; From East: Take A465 or A438 into Hereford Town Centre, then follow signs for Leominster (A49) into Edgar Street; From South: Take A49 or A45 into the Town Centre (then as East); From West: Take A438 into the Town Centre (then as East).

HUDDERSFIELD TOWN FC

Founded: 1908 (**Entered League:** 1910)
Former Names: None
Nickname: 'Terriers'
Ground: The Alfred McAlpine Stadium,
Leeds Road, Huddersfield   HD1 6PX
Record Attendance: 18,775 (6/5/95)
Pitch Size: 115 × 76 yards

Colours: Shirts – Blue and White Stripes
         Shorts – Blue
Telephone Nº: (01484) 420335
Ticket Office: (01484) 420335
Fax Number: (01484) 515122
Ground Capacity: 20,000 (All seats)

GARDNER MERCHANT
STAND
(Away)

GENERAL INFORMATION

Supporters Club: Mrs M. Procter, 23 Lincroft
Avenue, Dalton, Huddersfield   HD5 8DS
Telephone Nº: (01484) 420335
Car Parking: Car park for 1,100 cars adjacent
Coach Parking: Adjacent car park
Nearest Railway Station: Huddersfield (1¼ miles)
Nearest Bus Station: Huddersfield
Club Shop: At Ground
Opening Times: Weekdays 9.00am – 5.00pm and
Saturday Matchdays 9.00am – 3.00pm
Telephone Nº: (01484) 534867
Postal Sales: Yes
Nearest Police Station: Huddersfield (1 mile)
Police Telephone Nº: (01484) 422122

GROUND INFORMATION

Away Supporters' Entrances & Sections:
Gardner Merchant Stand

ADMISSION INFO (1996/97 PRICES)

Adult Seating: £10.00 to £14.00
Child Seating: £6.00 to £8.00
Programme Price: £1.50

DISABLED INFORMATION

Wheelchairs: 169 spaces in total for home and away
fans in the disabled sections, Riverside Stand and
Gardner Merchant Stand
Helpers: One helper admitted per wheelchair
Prices: Concessionary rates for disabled and helpers
Disabled Toilets: Available in the disabled sections
Commentaries are available for the blind
Are Bookings Necessary: No
Contact: (01484) 420335

Travelling Supporters' Information:
Routes: From North, East and West: Exit M62 at Junction 25 and take the A644 and A62 following Huddersfield
signs. Follow signs for the Alfred McAlpine Stadium; From South: Leave M1 at Junction 38 and follow A637/
A642 to Huddersfield. At the Ring Road, follow signs for the A62 to Alfred McAlpine Stadium.

HULL CITY FC

Founded: 1904 (Entered League: 1905)
Former Names: None
Nickname: 'Tigers'
Ground: Boothferry Park, Boothferry
Road, Hull   HU4 6EU
Record Attendance: 55,019 (26/2/49)
Pitch Size: 115 × 75 yards

Colours: Shirts – Black and Amber
  Shorts – Black
Telephone Nº: (01482) 351119
Ticket Office: (01482) 351119
Fax Number: (01482) 565752
Ground Capacity: 14,996
Seating Capacity: 5,495

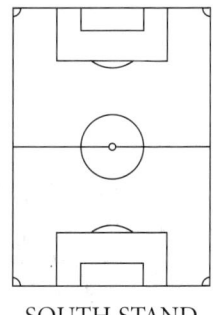

BOOTHFERRY ROAD
NORTH TERRACE
(Away)

NORTH ROAD
MAIN STAND

EAST STAND

SOUTH STAND

GENERAL INFORMATION

Supporters Club: F. Anholm, c/o The Club
Telephone Nº: (01482) 632987
Car Parking: Limited parking at the ground, street parking and schools
Coach Parking: At the ground
Nearest Railway Station: Hull Paragon (1½ miles)
Nearest Bus Station: Ferensway, Hull (1½ miles)
Club Shop: Paragon Square, Hull & at the ground
Opening Times: Paragon Square – Weekdays 9.30am to 4.30pm; Ground – Matchdays 10.00am – 4.30pm
Telephone Nº: (01482) 351119/328297
Postal Sales: Yes
Nearest Police Station: Central, Hull (2 miles)
Police Telephone Nº: (01482) 210031

GROUND INFORMATION

Away Supporters' Entrances & Sections:
North Stand turnstiles for North Terrace

ADMISSION INFO (1996/97 PRICES)

Adult Standing: £7.00
Adult Seating: £8.00 – £10.00
Child Standing: £3.00
Child Seating: £4.00 – £5.00
Programme Price: £1.50

DISABLED INFORMATION

Wheelchairs: 20 spaces in total for Home and Away fans in the disabled section, South East Corner
Helpers: One helper admitted per disabled person
Prices: Free of charge for disabled. Helpers £7.00
Disabled Toilets: One available within disabled area Commentaries are available for the blind
Are Bookings Necessary: No
Contact: (01482) 351119

Travelling Supporters' Information:
Routes: From North: Take A1 or A19 then A1079 into the City Centre and follow signs for Leeds (A63) into Anlaby Road. After 1 mile take the 1st exit at the roundabout into Boothferry Road; From West: Take M62 to A63 to Hull. Fork left after Ferriby Crest Motel to the Humber Bridge roundabout, then take the 1st exit to Boothferry Road – the ground is 1½ miles. Do NOT follow Clive Sullivan Way; From South: Non-scenic alternative route take M18 to M62 (then as West). Or use motorways M1 to M18, then M180 and follow signs over Humber Bridge (Toll), take 2nd exit at roundabout (A63) towards Boothferry Road (the ground is 1½ miles).

IPSWICH TOWN FC

Founded: 1887 (**Entered League:** 1938)	**Colours:** Shirts – Blue with White Sleeves
Former Names: None	Shorts – White
Nickname: 'Town'; 'Super Blues'	**Telephone Nº:** (01473) 219211
Ground: Portman Road, Ipswich	**Ticket Office:** (01473) 221133
IP1 2DA	**Fax Number:** (01473) 226835
Record Attendance: 38,010 (8/3/75)	**Ground Capacity:** 22,559 (All seats)
Pitch Size: 112 × 70 yards	

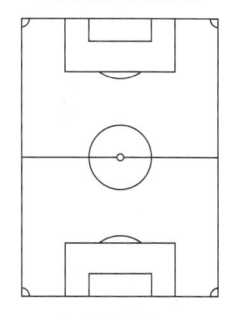

CHURCHMAN'S END
SOUTH STAND

PORTMAN ROAD (Away)
PORTMAN STAND

CONSTANTINE ROAD
PIONEER STAND

NORTH STAND
PORTMAN WALK

GENERAL INFORMATION

Supporters Club: Mr G. Dodson, c/o The Club
Telephone Nº: (01483) 219211
Car Parking: Portman Road and Portman Walk car parks
Coach Parking: Portman Walk
Nearest Railway Station: Ipswich (5 minutes walk)
Nearest Bus Station: Ipswich
Club Shop: At Ground
Opening Times: Weekdays and Matchdays 9.00am to 5.00pm
Telephone Nº: (01483) 214614
Postal Sales: Yes
Nearest Police Station: Civic Drive, Ipswich (5 minutes walk)
Police Telephone Nº: (01483) 55811

GROUND INFORMATION

Away Supporters' Entrances & Sections:
Portman Road turnstiles C and D

ADMISSION INFO (1996/97 PRICES)

Adult Seating: £11.00 – £18.00
Child Seating: £6.00 – £18.00
Programme Price: £1.50

DISABLED INFORMATION

Wheelchairs: 30 spaces + 50 seats for home fans, 6 spaces + 14 seats for away fans – in Pioneer Stand
Helpers: One helper admitted per disabled person
Prices: Free of charge for disabled. Helpers £11.00
Disabled Toilets: Adjacent to the disabled area
Commentaries are available for the blind
Are Bookings Necessary: Yes
Contact: (01483) 219211

Travelling Supporters' Information:
Routes: From North and West: Take A1214 from A14/A12 following signs for Ipswich West only. Proceed through Constable Country Hotel traffic lights and at the 2nd set of traffic lights turn right into West End Road. The ground is ¼ mile along on the left; From South: Follow signs for Ipswich West, then as North and West (above).

49

LEEDS UNITED FC

Founded: 1919 (**Entered League:** 1920)
Former Names: Formed after Leeds City FC were wound up for 'Irregular Practices'
Nickname: 'United'
Ground: Elland Road, Leeds LS11 0ES
Record Attendance: 57,892 (15/3/67)
Pitch Size: 117 × 76 yards

Colours: Shirts – White
        Shorts – White
Telephone Nº: (0113) 271-6037
Ticket Office: (0113) 271-0710
Fax Number: (0113) 270-6560
Ground Capacity: 40,204 (All seats)

ELLAND ROAD
SOUTH STAND

LOWFIELDS ROAD
EAST STAND

WEST STAND

REVIE STAND

GENERAL INFORMATION
Supporters Club: Eric Carlile, c/o The Club
Telephone Nº: (0113) 271-6037
Car Parking: Large car parks (adjacent)
Coach Parking: By Police direction
Nearest Railway Station: Leeds City (1½ miles)
Nearest Bus Station: Leeds City Centre – specials from Swinegate
Club Shop: At Ground
Opening Times: Weekdays 9.15am – 5.00pm, Matchdays 9.15am – kick-off
Telephone Nº: (0113) 270-6844
Postal Sales: Yes (send SAE)
Nearest Police Station: Holbeck, Leeds (3 miles)
Police Telephone Nº: (0113) 243-5353

GROUND INFORMATION
Away Supporters' Entrances & Sections:
South East Corner or South Stand

ADMISSION INFO (1995/96 PRICES)
Adult Seating: £14.00 – £25.00
Child Seating: £7.00 – £25.00
Programme Price: £1.50

DISABLED INFORMATION
Wheelchairs: 80 spaces in total in the disabled sections, West Stand and South West Corner
Helpers: One helper admitted per disabled person
Prices: Free of charge for disabled. Helpers £14.00
Disabled Toilets: One adjacent to each of the disabled sections
Commentaries via headphones in the West Stand
Are Bookings Necessary: Yes
Contact: (0113) 271-6037

Travelling Supporters' Information:
Routes: From North: Take A58 or A61 into the City Centre and follow signs to M621. Leave the Motorway after 1½ miles and exit the roundabout onto A643 into Elland Road; From North-East: Take A63 or A64 into the City Centre (then as North); From South: Take M1 to M621 (then as North); From West: Take M62 to M621 (then as North).

LEICESTER CITY FC

Founded: 1884 (**Entered League:** 1894)
Former Names: Leicester Fosse FC (1884-1919)
Nickname: 'Filberts'; 'Foxes'
Ground: City Stadium, Filbert Street, Leicester   LE2 7FL
Record Attendance: 47,298 (18/2/28)

Colours: Shirts – Blue
                   Shorts – Blue
Telephone Nº: (0116) 255-5000
Ticket Office: (0116) 291-5232
Fax Number: (0116) 247-0585
Pitch Size: 112 × 75 yards
Ground Capacity: 22,526 (All seats)

FILBERT STREET
NORTH STAND

CARLING STAND

(Away)

BROADMOOR STREET
EAST STAND

SOUTH STAND
SPION KOP
BLACK PAD

GENERAL INFORMATION
Supporters Club: C. Ginetta, c/o The Club
Telephone Nº: (0116) 255-5000
Car Parking: NCP Car Park (5 minutes walk)
Coach Parking: Sawday Street
Nearest Railway Station: Leicester (1 mile)
Nearest Bus Station: St. Margaret's (1 mile)
Club Shop: At Ground
Opening Times: Weekdays and Matchdays 9.00am to 5.30pm
Telephone Nº: (0116) 255-9455
Postal Sales: Yes
Nearest Police Station: Charles Street, Leicester
Police Telephone Nº: (0116) 253-0066

GROUND INFORMATION
Away Supporters' Entrances & Sections:
East Stand, Blocks T and U

ADMISSION INFO (1996/97 PRICES)
Adult Seating: £12.00 – £20.00
Child Seating: £6.00 – £10.00
Programme Price: £1.50

DISABLED INFORMATION
Wheelchairs: 58 spaces for home fans, 17 spaces for away fans in the disabled sections, South Stand Lower Tier and East Stand Block T
Helpers: One helper admitted per disabled person
Prices: Free of charge for disabled. Helpers £12.00
Disabled Toilets: Available in Carling Stand and East Stand Block T
Are Bookings Necessary: Yes
Contact: (0116) 255-5000

Travelling Supporters' Information:
Routes: From North: Take A46/A607 into the City Centre or exit M1 at Junction 22 for the City Centre, follow 'Rugby' signs into Almond Road, turn right at the end into Aylestone Road, turn left into Walnut Street and left again into Filbert Street; From East: Take A47 into the City Centre (then as North); From South: Exit M1 at Junction 21 and take A46, turn right ¾ mile after Railway Bridge into Upperton Road, then right into Filbert Street; From West: Take M69 to the City Centre (then as North).

LEYTON ORIENT FC

Founded: 1881 **(Entered League:** 1905)
Former Names: Glyn Cricket & Football
Club (1881/86); Eagle FC (1886/88);
Clapton Orient FC (1888/1946); Leyton
Orient FC (1946/66); Orient FC (1966/87)
Nickname: 'O's'
Record Attendance: 34,345 (21/1/64)

Colours: Shirts – Red; Shorts – White
Telephone N°: (0181) 539-2223
Ticket Office: (0181) 539-2223
Fax Number: (0181) 539-4390
Pitch Size: 115 × 80 yards
Ground Capacity: 17,065
Seating Capacity: 7,171

Ground: Leyton Stadium, Brisbane Road, Leyton, London E10 5NE

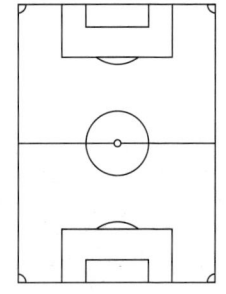

WINDSOR ROAD
NORTH TERRACE

OLIVER ROAD
WEST STAND

BRISBANE ROAD
MAIN STAND

(Closed for rebuilding)
BUCKINGHAM ROAD

GENERAL INFORMATION

Supporters Club: D. Dodd, c/o The Club
Telephone N°: (0181) 539-6156
Car Parking: NCP Brisbane Road & street parking
Coach Parking: By Police direction
Nearest Railway Station: Leyton Midland Road (½ mile)
Nearest Tube Station: Leyton (Central)
Club Shop: At Ground
Opening Times: Weekdays 10.00am – 4.30pm
Telephone N°: (0181) 539-2223
Postal Sales: Yes
Nearest Police Station: Francis Road, Leyton
Police Telephone N°: (0181) 556-8855

GROUND INFORMATION

Away Supporters' Entrances & Sections:
South Wing turnstiles for South Wing Section

ADMISSION INFO (1996/97 PRICES)

Adult Standing: £8.00
Adult Seating: £9.00 – £12.00
Child Standing: £4.00
Child Seating: £5.00 – £7.00
Programme Price: £1.50

DISABLED INFORMATION

Wheelchairs: 12 spaces in total for Home and Away fans in the disabled section, North Terrace
Helpers: One helper admitted per disabled person
Prices: Free of charge for Disabled and Helpers
Disabled Toilets: Available near the disabled section
Commentaries are available – contact Football in the Community: (0181) 556-5973
Are Bookings Necessary: Yes
Contact: (0181) 556-5973

Travelling Supporters' Information:
Routes: From North & West: Take A406 North Circular, follow signs for Chelmsford to Edmonton. After 2½ miles take 3rd exit at roundabout towards Leyton (A112). Pass railway station and turn right after ½ mile into Windsor Road and left into Brisbane Road; From East: Follow A12 to London then City for Leytonstone. Follow Hackney signs into Grove Road, cross Main Road into Ruckholt Road then turn right into Leyton High Road, turn left after ¼ mile into Buckingham Road and left into Brisbane Road; From South: Take A102M through Blackwall Tunnel, follow signs for Newmarket (A102) to join A11 to Stratford, then follow signs for Stratford Station into Leyton Road to railway station (then as North).

LINCOLN CITY FC

Founded: 1883 (**Entered League:** 1892)
Former Names: None
Nickname: 'Red Imps'
Ground: Sincil Bank, Lincoln   LN5 8LD
Record Attendance: 23, 196 (15/11/67)
Pitch Size: 110 × 76 yards

Colours: Shirts – Red and White Stripes
 Shorts – Black
Telephone Nº: (01522) 522224
Ticket Office: (01522) 522224
Fax Number: (01522) 520564
Ground Capacity: 10, 918
Seating Capacity: 9,246

STACEY WEST STAND

SINCIL BANK LINPAVE STAND (Away)

ST. ANDREW'S STAND

SOUTH PARK STAND

GENERAL INFORMATION
Supporters Club: c/o The Club
Telephone Nº: (01522) 522224
Car Parking: Adjacent to the ground (£2.00)
Coach Parking: South Common (300 yards)
Nearest Railway Station: Lincoln Central
Club Shop: At the ground – St. Andrew's Stand
Opening Times: Weekdays & Matchdays 9.00am to 5.00pm
Telephone Nº: (01522) 522224
Postal Sales: Yes
Nearest Police Station: West Parade, Lincoln (1½ miles)
Police Telephone Nº: (01522) 529911

GROUND INFORMATION
Away Supporters' Entrances & Sections:
Linpave Stand turnstiles 17-21

ADMISSION INFO (1996/97 PRICES)
Adult Standing: £6.00
Adult Seating: £6.00 – £8.00
Child Standing: £4.50
Child Seating: £4.50 – £6.00
Programme Price: £1.30

DISABLED INFORMATION
Wheelchairs: 62 spaces in total for Home and Away fans in the disabled section, adjacent to turnstile 23
Helpers: One helper admitted per disabled person
Prices: Free of charge for Disabled and Helpers
Disabled Toilets: Adjacent to disabled area
Are Bookings Necessary: Yes
Contact: (01522) 522224

Travelling Supporters' Information:
Routes: From East: Take A46 or A158 into the City Centre following Newark (A46) signs into High Street and take next left (Scorer Street and Cross Street) for the ground; From North & West: Take A15 or A57 into the City Centre, then as East; From South: Take A1 to A46 for the City Centre, then into High Street and turn right into Scorer Street, then right again into Cross Street for the ground.

LIVERPOOL FC

Founded: 1892 (**Entered League:** 1893)
Former Names: None
Nickname: 'Reds'
Ground: Anfield Road, Liverpool
L4 0TH
Record Attendance: 61,905 (2/2/52)
Pitch Size: 110 × 74 yards

Colours: Shirts – Red + White Markings
Shorts – Red + White Markings
Telephone Nº: (0151) 263-2361
Ticket Office: (0151) 260-8680;
(0151) 263-5727 (Credit Card bookings)
Fax Number: (0151) 260-8813
Ground Capacity: 41,000 (All seats)

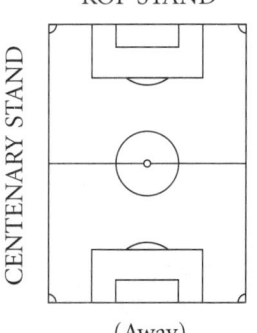

WALTON BRECK ROAD
KOP STAND

CENTENARY STAND

PADDOCK ENCLOSURE

LOTHAIR ROAD
MAIN STAND

(Away)
ANFIELD ROAD STAND

GENERAL INFORMATION
Supporters Club: Liverpool International
Supporters' Club, c/o Liverpool FC
Telephone Nº: (0151) 263-2361
Car Parking: Stanley Park car park (adjacent)
Coach Parking: Priory Road and Pinehurst Avenue
Nearest Railway Station: Kirkdale (¾ mile)
Nearest Bus Station: Paradise Street, Liverpool
Club Shop: At Ground
Opening Times: Monday to Saturday 9.30am –
5.00pm
Telephone Nº: (0151) 263-1760
Postal Sales: Yes
Nearest Police Station: Walton Lane (1½ miles)
Police Telephone Nº: (0151) 709-6010

GROUND INFORMATION
Away Supporters' Entrances & Sections:
Anfield Road

ADMISSION INFO (1996/97 PRICES)
Adult Seating: £17.00
Kop Seating: £14.00
Programme Price: £1.70

DISABLED INFORMATION
Wheelchairs: 40 spaces for home fans only in the
Paddock Enclosure and Kop Stand
Helpers: One helper admitted per wheelchair
Prices: £3.00 per disabled fan. £17 or £14 per helper
Disabled Toilets: One available in the Paddock, two
in the Kop Stand
Commentaries are available for the blind
Are Bookings Necessary: Yes
Contact: (0151) 260-8680

Travelling Supporters' Information:
Routes: From North: Exit M6 at Junction 28 and follow Liverpool A58 signs into Walton Hall Avenue, pass
Stanley Park and turn left into Anfield Road; From South and East: Take M62 to the end of the motorway, then
turn right into Queen's Drive (A5058) and turn left after 3 miles into Utting Avenue. After 1 mile, turn right into
Anfield Road; From North Wales: Take the Mersey Tunnel into the City Centre and follow signs for Preston
(A580) into Walton Hall Avenue. Turn right into Anfield Road before Stanley Park.

LUTON TOWN FC

Founded: 1885 (**Entered League:** 1897)
Former Names: Formed by amalgamation of Wanderers FC and Excelsior FC
Nickname: 'Hatters'
Ground: Kenilworth Road Stadium, 1 Maple Road, Luton   LU4 8AW
Record Attendance: 30,069 (4/3/59)

Colours: Shirts – white/royal blue/orange
Shorts – blue/orange/white trim
Telephone Nº: (01582) 411622
Ticket Office: (01582) 416976
Fax Number: (01582) 405070
Pitch Size: 110 × 72 yards
Ground Capacity: 9,970 (All seats)

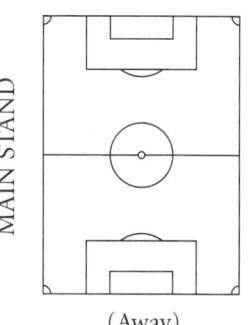

KENILWORTH ROAD
KENILWORTH STAND

MAPLE ROAD
MAIN STAND

BEECH HILL PATH
EXECUTIVE BOXES

(Away)
OAK STAND
OAK ROAD

GENERAL INFORMATION

Supporters Club: c/o Club Ticket Office
Telephone Nº: (01582) 416976
Car Parking: Street Parking
Coach Parking: Luton Bus Station
Nearest Railway Station: Luton (1 mile)
Nearest Bus Station: Bute Street, Luton
Club Shop: Kenilworth Road Forecourt
Opening Times: 10.00am – 4.00pm
Telephone Nº: (01582) 411622
Postal Sales: Yes
Nearest Police Stat'n: Buxton Road, Luton (¾ mile)
Police Telephone Nº: (01582) 401212

GROUND INFORMATION

Away Supporters' Entrances & Sections:
Oak Road for the Oak Stand

ADMISSION INFO (1996/97 PRICES)

Adult Seating: £8.00 – £15.50
Child Seating: £5.50 – £8.00
Programme Price: £1.50
Note: Lower prices apply when tickets are purchased at least 14 days before the game and different prices apply for certain cup games.

DISABLED INFORMATION

Wheelchairs: 15 spaces in total for Home and Away fans in the disabled section in the Main Stand
Helpers: One helper admitted per disabled person
Prices: Free of charge for Disabled and Helpers
Disabled Toilets: Available adjacent to disabled area
Commentaries are available for the blind
Are Bookings Necessary: Yes
Contact: (01582) 411622

Travelling Supporters' Information:
Routes: From North and West: Exit M1 at Junction 11 and follow signs for Luton (A505) into Dunstable Road. Follow the one-way system and turn right back towards Dunstable, take the first left into Oak Road; From South and East: Exit M1 at Junction 10 (or A6/A612) into Luton Town Centre and follow signs into Dunstable Road. After the railway bridge, take the sixth turning on the left into Oak Road.

MANCHESTER CITY FC

Founded: 1887 **(Entered League:** 1892)
Former Names: Ardwick FC (1897-94)
Nickname: 'Citizens'; 'City'; 'Blues'
Ground: Maine Road, Moss Side,
Manchester M14 7WN
Record Attendance: 84,569 (3/3/34)
Pitch Size: 117 × 76 yards

Colours: Shirts – Sky Blue
Shorts – White
Telephone Nº: (0161) 224-5000
Ticket Office: (0161) 226-2224
Credit Card Bookings: (0161) 227-9229
Fax Number: (0161) 248-8449
Ground Capacity: 31,500 (All seats)

UMBRO STAND

KIPPAX STAND

MAINE ROAD
MAIN STAND

(Away)
NORTH STAND
(CLAREMONT ROAD)

GENERAL INFORMATION

Supporters Club: c/o Frank Horrocks, Manchester City Supporters' Club, Maine Road, Manchester
Telephone Nº: (0161) 226-5047
Car Parking: Street Parking and Local Schools
Coach Parking: Kippax Street car park
Nearest Railway Station: Manchester Piccadilly (2½ miles)
Nearest Bus Station: Chorlton Street
Club Shop: At Ground
Opening Times: Monday to Saturday 9.00am – 5.00pm and Matchdays 9.00am – 6.00pm
Telephone Nº: (0161) 226-4824
Postal Sales: Yes
Nearest Police Station: Platt Lane, Moss Side
Police Telephone Nº: (0161) 872-5050

GROUND INFORMATION

Away Supporters' Entrances & Sections:
North Stand

ADMISSION INFO (1996/97 PRICES)

Adult Seating: £10.00 – £16.00
Child Seating: £6.00 (Family Stand)
Programme Price: £1.60

DISABLED INFORMATION

Wheelchairs: 56 spaces in total for Home and Away fans in the disabled section, Umbro Stand
Helpers: One helper admitted per wheelchair
Prices: Free of charge for disabled. Helpers £4.00
Disabled Toilets: 7 available in the Umbro Stand Hospital commentaries are available for 11 blind fans + helpers – in the Main Stand, G Block
Are Bookings Necessary: Yes
Contact: (0161) 226-1191

Travelling Supporters' Information:
Routes: From North & West: Take M61 & M63 exit Junction 9 following Manchester signs (A5103). Turn right at crossroads (2¾ miles) into Claremont Road. After ¼ mile turn left into Maine Road; From South: Exit M6 Junction 19 to A556 and M56 Junction 3 following Manchester signs (A5103) (then as North); From East: Exit M62 onto M602 Salford Motorway. Follow to end then take right hand lane and continue into Manchester along A57. Pass Sainsburys and go under railway bridge heading for Mancunian Way. After 2 roundabouts join Mancunian Way (elevated road) but leave at first exit and go under elevated section to roundabout then straight across. Follow road along past Dental Hospital into Lloyd Street and continue along to the ground.

MANCHESTER UNITED FC

Founded: 1878 (**Entered League:** 1892)
Former Names: Newton Heath LYR FC
(1878-92); Newton Heath FC (1892-1902)
Nickname: 'Red Devils'
Ground: Sir Matt Busby Way,
Old Trafford, Manchester   M16 0RA
Record Attendance: 76,962 (25/3/39)

Colours: Shirts – Red
      Shorts – White
Telephone Nº: (0161) 930-1968
Ticket Office: (0161) 872-0199
Fax Number: (0161) 896-5502
Pitch Size: 116 × 76 yards
Ground Capacity: 55,300 (All seats)

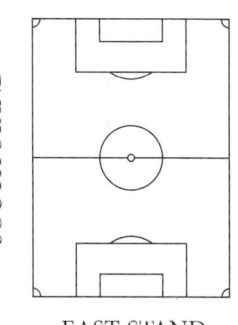

GENERAL INFORMATION

Supporters Club: Barry Moorhouse, c/o The Club
Telephone Nº: (0161) 872-5208
Car Parking: Lancashire Cricket Ground (1,200 cars)
Coach Parking: By Police direction
Nearest Railway Station: At the ground
Nearest Bus Station: Chorlton Street
Nearest Metro Station: Old Trafford
Club Shop: At Ground
Opening Times: Weekdays 9.30am – 5.00pm;
Matchdays 9.30am – 3.00pm; Sundays 10.00am –
4.00pm; Non-match Saturdays 9.30am – 4.00pm
Telephone Nº: (0161) 872-3398
Postal Sales: Yes
Nearest Police Stat'n: Talbot Road, Stretford (½ ml)
Police Telephone Nº: (0161) 872-5050

GROUND INFORMATION

Away Supporters' Entrances & Sections:
North Stand

ADMISSION INFO (1996/97 PRICES)

Adult Seating: £12.00 – £18.00
Child Seating: £6.00 – £8.00
Programme Price: £1.50

DISABLED INFORMATION

Wheelchairs: 72 spaces in total for Home and Away
fans in the disabled section – in front of 'L' Stand
Helpers: One helper admitted per disabled person
Prices: Free of charge for Disabled and Helpers
Disabled Toilets: Located near the disabled section
Commentaries are available for the blind
Are Bookings Necessary: Yes
Contact: (0161) 872-1661

Travelling Supporters' Information:
Routes: From North and West: Take M61 to M63 and exit Junction 4 following Manchester (A5081) signs. Turn right after 2½ miles into Warwick Road for the ground; From South: Exit M6 at Junction 19 and take Stockport (A556) road then Altrincham (A56). From Altrincham follow Manchester signs and turn left into Warwick Road after 6 miles; From East: Exit M62 at Junction 17 and take A56 to Manchester. Follow signs for the South then signs for Chester (Chester Road). Turn right into Warwick Road after 2 miles.

MANSFIELD TOWN FC

Founded: 1891 (**Entered League:** 1931)
Former Names: Manfield Wesleyans FC
(1891-1905)
Nickname: 'Stags'
Ground: Field Mill Ground, Quarry
Lane, Mansfield, Notts.
Record Attendance: 24,467 (10/1/53)

Colours: Shirts – Amber and Blue Stripes
Shorts – White
Telephone Nº: (01623) 23567
Ticket Office: (01623) 23567
Fax Number: (01623) 25014
Pitch Size: 115 × 70 yards
Ground Capacity: 7,073
Seating Capacity: 2,275

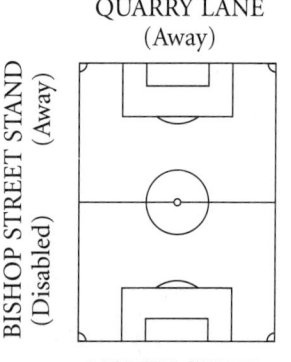

QUARRY LANE
(Away)

BISHOP STREET STAND (Away)

BISHOP STREET (Disabled)

WEST STAND

NORTH STAND

GENERAL INFORMATION

Supporters Club: c/o Miss T. Brown, 55 Rosecroft
Drive, Edwards Lane Estate, Nottingham
Telephone Nº: –
Car Parking: Large car park at the ground
Coach Parking: Adjacent to the ground
Nearest Railway Station: Mansfield Alfreton
Parkway – 9 miles (no public transport)
Nearest Bus Station: Mansfield
Club Shop: At Ground
Opening Times: Weekdays and Matchdays 9.00am
– 5.00pm
Telephone Nº: (01623) 658070
Postal Sales: Yes
Nearest Police Station: Mansfield (¼ mile)
Police Telephone Nº: (01623) 22622

GROUND INFORMATION

Away Supporters' Entrances & Sections:
Quarry Lane turnstiles for Quarry Lane End (open)

ADMISSION INFO (1996/97 PRICES)

Adult Standing: £8.00
Adult Seating: £10.00
Child Standing: £3.00
Child Seating: £5.00
Programme Price: £1.30

DISABLED INFORMATION

Wheelchairs: 40 spaces in total accommodated in
the disabled section – North End of Bishop Street
Helpers: Admitted
Prices: Free for the disabled. Helpers full price
Disabled Toilets: Adjacent to the disabled section
Are Bookings Necessary: Not usually
Contact: (01623) 23567

Travelling Supporters' Information:
Routes: From North: Exit M1 at Junction 29 and take A617 to Mansfield. After 6¼ miles turn right at the Leisure
Centre into Rosemary Street. Carry on to Quarry Lane and turn right; From South and West: Exit M1 at Junction 28 and take A38 to Mansfield. After 6½ miles turn right at the crossroads into Belvedere Street then turn right after ¼ mile into Quarry Lane; From East: Take A617 to Rainworth, turn left at the crossroads after 3 miles into Windsor Road and turn right at the end into Nottingham Road, then left into Quarry Lane.

MIDDLESBROUGH FC

Founded: 1876 (**Entered League:** 1892)
Former Names: None
Nickname: 'Boro'
Ground: Cellnet Riverside Stadium,
Middlesbrough, Cleveland   TS6 3RS
Record Attendance: 53,596 (27/12/49)
Pitch Size: 115 × 75 yards

Colours: Shirts – Red with White Yoke
Shorts – White
Telephone Nº: (01642) 227227
Ticket Office: (01642) 207014
Fax Number: (01642) 248450
Ground Capacity: 30,256 (All seats)

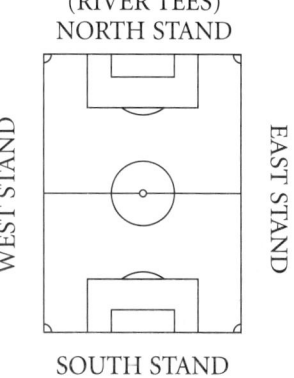

(RIVER TEES)
NORTH STAND

WEST STAND

EAST STAND

SOUTH STAND

GENERAL INFORMATION

Supporters Club: Simon Bolton, c/o The Club
Telephone Nº: (01642) 470512
Car Parking: 1,250 spaces (Season Ticket holders only)
Coach Parking: At the ground
Nearest Railway Station: Middlesbrough (¼ mile)
Nearest Bus Station: Middlesbrough
Club Shop: At Ground
Opening Times: Weekdays 9.30am – 5.00pm;
Saturdays 10.00am – 12.00pm + Matchdays
Telephone Nº: (01642) 207005
Postal Sales: Yes
Nearest Police Station: Dunning Street (1 mile)
Police Telephone Nº: (01642) 248184

GROUND INFORMATION

Away Supporters' Entrances & Sections:
South Stand turnstiles for the South Stand

ADMISSION INFO (1996/97 PRICES)

Adult Seating: £12.50 – £19.00
Child Seating: £7.00 – £19.00
Programme Price: £1.50
Note: It is expected that only Season Ticket holders will be admitted in 1996/97

DISABLED INFORMATION

Wheelchairs: 170 spaces in total for home and away fans in the disabled areas, West and South Stands
Helpers: One helper admitted per disabled person
Prices: £9.50 Upper level, £7.50 Lower level for disabled and helpers
Disabled Toilets: Available in West & South Stands
Commentaries are available – 40 headsets
Are Bookings Necessary: Yes
Contact: (01642) 227227

Travelling Supporters' Information:
Routes: From North: Take A19 across flyover and join A66 (Eastbound). At the end of the flyover, turn left at North Ormesby roundabout. The ground is 200 metres down the road; From South: Take A1 and A19 to the junction with A66 (Eastbound). After the flyover, turn left at the North Ormesby roundabout.

MILLWALL FC

Founded: 1885 (**Entered League:** 1920)
Former Names: Millwall Rovers FC (1885-93); Millwall Athletic FC (1893-1925)
Nickname: 'Lions'
Ground: The Den, Zampa Road, London SE16 3LN
Record Attendance: 20,093 (10/1/94)

Colours: Shirts – Blue
         Shorts – White
Telephone Nº: (0171) 232-1222
Ticket Office: (0171) 231-9999
Fax Number: (0171) 231-3663
Pitch Size: 112 × 74 yards
Ground Capacity: 20, 146 (All seats)

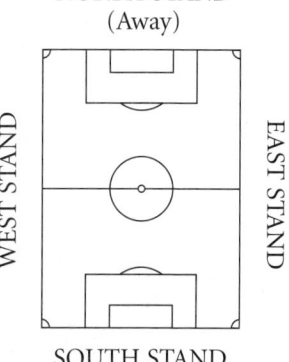

NORTH STAND
(Away)

WEST STAND

EAST STAND

SOUTH STAND

GENERAL INFORMATION
Supporters Club: None
Telephone Nº: –
Car Parking: Juno Way
Coach Parking: Adjacent to ground
Nearest Railway Station: New Cross Gate/South Bermondsey (½ mile)
Nearest Tube Station: New Cross Gate/Surrey Quays (½ mile)
Club Shop: Next to Stadium
Opening Times: Daily 9.30am – 4.30pm
Telephone Nº: (0171) 231-9845
Postal Sales: Yes
Nearest Police Station: Deptford/Lewisham (1 mile)
Police Telephone Nº: (0171) 679-9217

GROUND INFORMATION
Away Supporters' Entrances & Sections:
North East Stand turnstiles 31-36 for North Stand

ADMISSION INFO (1996/97 PRICES)
Adult Seating: £10.00 – £18.00
Child Seating: £5.00
Programme Price: £1.70

DISABLED INFORMATION
Wheelchairs: 200 spaces in total for home and away fans in the disabled section, West Stand
Helpers: One helper admitted per disabled person
Prices: Free of charge for disabled. Helpers £10.00
Disabled Toilets: 17 toilets available around the Stadium
Commentaries are available for the blind
Are Bookings Necessary: Yes
Contact: (0171) 232-1222

Travelling Supporters' Information:
Routes: From North: Follow City signs from M1/A1 then signs for Shoreditch & Whitechapel. Follow Ring Road signs for Dover, cross over Tower Bridge and after 1 mile take 1st exit at the roundabout onto A2. From Elephant and Castle take A2 (New Kent Road) into Old Kent Road and turn left after 4 miles at Canterbury Arms pub into Ilderton Road then follow Surrey Canal Road to Zampa Road; From South: Take A20 & A21 following signs to London. At New Cross follow signs for Stadium; From East: Take A2 to New Cross (then as South); From West: From M4 & M3 follow South Circular (A205) then follow signs for Clapham, City (A3) then Camberwell to New Cross and then as from the South.

NEWCASTLE UNITED FC

Founded: 1882 (**Entered League:** 1893)
Former Names: Newcastle East End FC
(1882-92) joined Newcastle West End FC
Nickname: 'Magpies'
Ground: St. James Park, Newcastle-
Upon-Tyne   NE1 4ST
Record Attendance: 68,386 (3/9/30)

Colours: Shirts – Black and White Stripes
Shorts – Black
Telephone Nº: (0191) 201-8400
Ticket Office: (0191) 261-1571
Fax Number: (0191) 201-8600
Pitch Size: 110 × 73 yards
Ground Capacity: 36,610 (All seats)

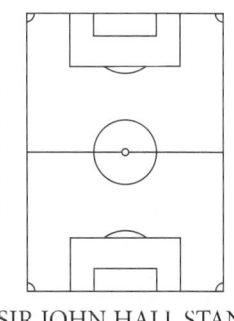

STRAWBERRY PLACE
EXHIBITION STAND

ST. JAMES STREET
EAST STAND

BARRACK ROAD
MILBURN STAND

SIR JOHN HALL STAND

GENERAL INFORMATION
Supporters Club: None
Telephone Nº: –
Car Parking: Street Parking
Coach Parking: By Police direction
Nearest Railway Station: Newcastle Central (¼ ml)
Nearest Bus Station: Gallowgate (¼ mile)
Club Shop: At ground, Eldon Square, Haymarket
and MetroCentre
Opening Times: All shops are open Monday to
Saturday 9.00am – 5.00pm; Eldon open until
8.00pm on Thursdays; MetroCentre open until at
least 7.00pm Monday to Saturday
Telephone Nº: (0191) 201-8401
Postal Sales: Yes   **Phone:** (0191) 262-6878
Nearest Police Station: Market Street, Newcastle
Police Telephone Nº: (0191) 232-3451

GROUND INFORMATION
Away Supporters' Entrances & Sections:
North East Corner for Sir John Hall Stand

ADMISSION INFO (1995/96 PRICES)
Adult Seating: £12.00 – £20.00
Child Seating: £6.00 – £14.00
Programme Price: £1.50
Note: It is expected than only Season Ticket holders
will be admitted in 1996/97

DISABLED INFORMATION
Wheelchairs: 95 spaces in total in the disabled
areas, Sir John Hall Stand and Exhibition Stand
Helpers: One helper admitted per disabled person
Prices: Prices available on application
Disabled Toilets: Available in Sir John Hall Stand
Commentaries are available for 20 blind supporters
Are Bookings Necessary: Yes
Contact: (0191) 201-8400

Travelling Supporters' Information:
Routes: From North: Follow A1 into Newcastle, then Hexham signs into Percy Street. Turn right into Leazes Park
Road; From South: Take A1M, then after Birtley Granada Services take A69 Gateshead Western Bypass (bear left on
Motorway). Follow Airport signs for approx. 3 miles then take A692 (Newcastle) sign, crossing the Redheugh Bridge.
At roundabout, take 3rd exit (Blenheim Street). Proceed over two sets of traffic lights crossing Westmorland Road,
Westgate Road then left into Bath Lane. Over traffic lights to roundabout and take 3rd exit into Barrack Road; From
West: Take A69 towards City Centre. Pass Newcastle General Hospital. At traffic lights after Hospital turn left into
Brighton Grove. After 70 yards turn right into Stanhope Street, proceed into Barrack Road.

NORTHAMPTON TOWN FC

Founded: 1897 (**Entered League:** 1920)
Former Names: None
Nickname: 'Cobblers'
Ground: Sixfields Stadium, Upton Way,
Northampton   NN5 4EG
Record Attendance: 7,461 (15/10/94)
Pitch Size: 112 × 75 yards

Colours: Shirts – Claret
            Shorts – White
Telephone Nº: (01604) 757773
Ticket Office: (01604) 588338
Fax Number: (01604) 751613
Ground Capacity: 7,653 (All seats)

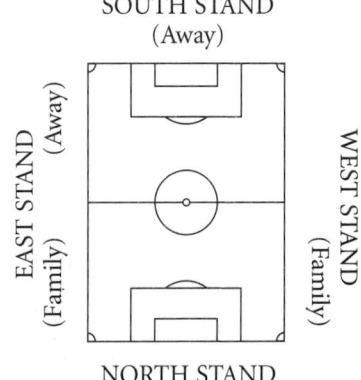

SOUTH STAND
(Away)

EAST STAND
(Away)

WEST STAND
(Family)

EAST STAND
(Family)

NORTH STAND

GENERAL INFORMATION

Supporters Club: Northampton Supporters Trust,
10 Ainsdale Close, Links View, Northampton
Telephone Nº: –
Car Parking: At the ground
Coach Parking: At the ground
Nearest Railway Station: Northampton Castle
(2 miles)
Nearest Bus Station: Greyfriars
Club Shop: At Ground
Opening Times: Weekdays 10.00am – 4.00pm and
Matchdays 9.00am – 6.00pm
Telephone Nº: (01604) 757773
Postal Sales: Yes
Nearest Police Station: Campbell Square,
Northampton
Police Telephone Nº: (01604) 700700

GROUND INFORMATION

Away Supporters' Entrances & Sections:
South Stand Entrance for South and East Stands

ADMISSION INFO (1996/97 PRICES)

Adult Seating: £8.50 – £11.00
Child Seating: £4.00 – £7.50
Programme Price: £1.50
In addition to various combinations of adults and
children, concessions also apply

DISABLED INFORMATION

Wheelchairs: 80 spaces in total for Home and Away
fans in various areas of the ground
Helpers: One helper admitted per disabled person
Prices: £4.00 each for disabled fans and helpers
Disabled Toilets: Available by the disabled areas
Commentaries are available for the blind
Are Bookings Necessary: Yes
Contact: (01604) 588338

Travelling Supporters' Information:
Routes: From All Parts: Exit the M1 at Junction 15A following the signs for Sixfields Leisure onto Upton Way –
the ground is approximately 2 miles.

NORWICH CITY FC

Founded: 1902 (**Entered League:** 1920)
Former Names: None
Nickname: 'Canaries'
Ground: Carrow Road, Norwich
NR1 1JE
Record Attendance: 43,984 (30/3/63)
Pitch Size: 114 × 74 yards

Colours: Shirts – Yellow
              Shorts – Green
Telephone Nº: (01603) 760760
Ticket Office: (01603) 761661
Fax Number: (01603) 619011
Ground Capacity: 21,972 (All seats)

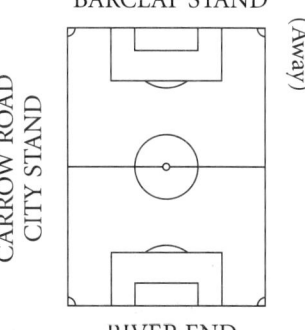

CARROW ROAD
BARCLAY STAND

CARROW ROAD
CITY STAND

SOUTH STAND (Disabled)
(Away)

RIVER END
STAND

GENERAL INFORMATION

Supporters Club: c/o Kevan Platt, Club Canary, Carrow Road, Norwich
Telephone Nº: (01603) 760760
Car Parking: City Centre car parks (nearby)
Coach Parking: Lower Clarence Road
Nearest Railway Station: Norwich Thorpe (1 mile)
Nearest Bus Station: Surrey Street, Norwich
Club Shop: In City Stand
Opening Times: Weekdays and Matchdays 9.00am – 5.00pm
Telephone Nº: (01603) 761125
Postal Sales: Yes
Nearest Police Stat'n: Bethel Street, Norwich (1 ml)
Police Telephone Nº: (01603) 768769

GROUND INFORMATION

Away Supporters' Entrances & Sections:
Turnstiles 1-3 – Barclay End for South Stand Blocks F, G, H and J

ADMISSION INFO (1996/97 PRICES)

Adult Seating: £10.00 – £15.00
Child Seating: £5.00 – £10.00
Programme Price: £1.50
Note: Prices vary according to the category of the game

DISABLED INFORMATION

Wheelchairs: 34 spaces for home fans and 6 for away fans in South Stand/River End corner
Helpers: One helper admitted per disabled person
Prices: Free of charge for disabled. Helpers £5.00 – £10.00 according to match category
Disabled Toilets: One available within disabled area
Are Bookings Necessary: Yes
Contact: (01603) 761661

Travelling Supporters' Information:
Routes: From South: Take A11 or A140 and turn right onto A47 towards Great Yarmouth & Lowestoft, take A146 Norwich/Lowestoft sliproad, turn left towards Norwich and follow road signs for the Football Ground; From West: Take A47 on to A146 Norwich/Lowestoft slip road. Turn left towards Norwich, follow the road signs for the Football Ground.

NOTTINGHAM FOREST FC

Founded: 1865 (**Entered League:** 1892)
Former Names: None
Nickname: 'Reds'; 'Forest'
Ground: City Ground, Nottingham, NG2 5FJ
Record Attendance: 49,945 (28/10/67)
Pitch Size: 115 × 78 yards

Colours: Shirts – Red
Shorts – White
Telephone Nº: (0115) 952-6000
Ticket Office: (0115) 952-6002
Fax Number: (0115) 952-6003
Ground Capacity: 30,602 (All seats)

BRIDGFORD STAND
(Away)

EXECUTIVE STAND

PAVILION ROAD
MAIN STAND

TRENT END
STAND

GENERAL INFORMATION

Supporters Club: Mr B. Tewson, c/o The Club
Telephone Nº: (0115) 952-6000
Car Parking: East car park (300 cars) & street parking
Coach Parking: East car park, Meadow Lane
Nearest Railway Station: Nottingham Midland (½ mile)
Nearest Bus Station: Victoria Street/Broadmarsh Centre
Club Shop: At Ground
Opening Times: Weekdays 9.00am – 5.00pm; Matchdays 9.00am – 3.00pm
Telephone Nº: (0115) 952-6026
Postal Sales: Yes
Nearest Police Station: Rectory Road, West Bridgford (1 mile)
Police Telephone Nº: (0115) 948-1888

GROUND INFORMATION

Away Supporters' Entrances & Sections:
Entrances via East car park for Bridgford Stand

ADMISSION INFO (1996/97 PRICES)

Adult Seating: £18.00 – £20.00
Child Seating: £9.00 (Family Section only)
Programme Price: £1.50

DISABLED INFORMATION

Wheelchairs: 50 spaces in total for Home and Away fans in the disabled area, in front of Executive Stand
Helpers: One helper admitted per disabled person
Prices: Free of charge for disabled. Helpers £18.00
Disabled Toilets: Available in the Executive Stand
Are Bookings Necessary: Yes
Contact: (0115) 952-6000

Travelling Supporters' Information:
Routes: From North: Exit M1 at Junction 26 following Nottingham signs (A610) then Melton Mowbray an Trent Bridge (A606) signs. Cross River Trent, left into Radcliffe Road then left into Colwick Road for ground; From South: Exit M1 at Junction 24 following signs for Nottingham (South) to Trent Bridge. Turn right into Radcliffe Road then left into Colwick Road; From East: Take A52 to West Bridgford, turn right into Colwick Road; From West: Take A52 into Nottingham following signs for Melton Mowbray and Trent Bridge, cross Rover Trent (then as North).

NOTTS COUNTY FC

Founded: 1862 (**Entered League:** 1888)
Former Names: None
Nickname: 'Magpies'
Ground: Meadow Lane, Nottingham, NG2 3HJ
Record Attendance: 47,310 (12/3/55)
Pitch Size: 117 × 76 yards

Colours: Shirts – Black and White Stripes
Shorts – Black
Telephone Nº: (0115) 952-9000
Ticket Office: (0115) 955-7210
Fax Number: (0115) 955-3994
Ground Capacity: 20,300 (All seats)

MEADOW LANE
FAMILY STAND

JIMMY SIRRELL STAND — Disabled

DEREK PAVIS STAND

THE KOP STAND (Away)
CATTLE MARKET ROAD

GENERAL INFORMATION

Supporters Club: P. Dennis, c/o The Club
Telephone Nº: (0115) 955-7255
Car Parking: British Waterways, Meadow Lane
Coach Parking: Incinerator Road (Cattle Market Corner)
Nearest Railway Station: Nottingham Midland (½ mile)
Nearest Bus Station: Broadmarsh Centre
Club Shop: At Ground
Opening Times: Weekdays and Matchdays 9.00am – 5.30pm; Other Saturdays 9.00am – 12.00pm
Telephone Nº: (0115) 952-9000
Postal Sales: Yes
Nearest Police Station: Station Street, Nottingham
Police Telephone Nº: (0115) 948-1888

GROUND INFORMATION

Away Supporters' Entrances & Sections:
Cattle Market Corner for The Kop Stand

ADMISSION INFO (1996/97 PRICES)

Adult Seating: £10.00 – £14.00
Child Seating: £5.00 – £7.00
Programme Price: £1.30

DISABLED INFORMATION

Wheelchairs: 100 spaces in total in the disabled area, County Road/Meadow Lane End corner
Helpers: One helper admitted per disabled fan
Prices: Free for the disabled. Helpers full price
Disabled Toilets: Available next to the disabled area
Are Bookings Necessary: Yes
Contact: (0115) 955-7210

Travelling Supporters' Information:
Routes: From North: Exit M1 Junction 26 following Nottingham signs (A610) then Melton Mowbray and Trent Bridge (A606) signs. Before River Trent turn left into Meadow Lane; From South: Exit M1 Junction 24 following signs Nottingham (South) to Trent Bridge, cross River and follow one-way system to the right, then turn left and right at traffic lights then second right into Meadow Lane; From East: Take A52 to West Bridgford/Trent Bridge, cross River and follow one-way system to the right then turn left and right at traffic lights, then second right into Meadow Lane; From West: Take A52 into Nottingham following signs for Melton Mowbray and Trent Bridge, before River Trent turn left into Meadow Lane.

OLDHAM ATHLETIC FC

Founded: 1895 (**Entered League:** 1907)
Former Names: Pine Villa FC (1895-99)
Nickname: 'Latics'
Ground: Boundary Park, Oldham,
OL1 2PA
Record Attendance: 47,671 (25/1/30)
Pitch Size: 110 × 74 yards

Colours: Shirts – Blue
 Shorts – Blue
Telephone Nº: (0161) 624-4972 (24 hrs)
Ticket Office: (0161) 624-4972
Fax Number: (0161) 627-5915
Ground Capacity: 13,700 (All seats)

ROCHDALE ROAD
STAND   (Away)

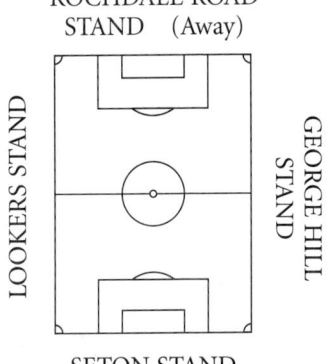

LOOKERS STAND

GEORGE HILL STAND

SETON STAND

GENERAL INFORMATION

Supporters Club: Dave Cunningham, c/o The Club
Telephone Nº: (0161) 624-4972
Car Parking: Lookers Stand car park (1,000 cars)
Coach Parking: At the ground
Nearest Railway Station: Oldham Werneth (1½ ml)
Nearest Bus Station: Oldham Mumps (2 miles)
Club Shop: At Ground
Opening Times: Mondays to Saturdays 9.00am –
5.00pm
Telephone Nº: (0161) 652-0966
Postal Sales: Yes
Nearest Police Station: Chadderton
Police Telephone Nº: (0161) 624-0444

GROUND INFORMATION

Away Supporters' Entrances & Sections:
Rochdale Road turnstiles for Rochdale Road seating

ADMISSION INFO (1996/97 PRICES)

Adult Seating: £7.50 – £13.00   (Away fans £12.00)
Child Seating: £5.00   (Away fans £5.00)
Programme Price: £1.50

DISABLED INFORMATION

Wheelchairs: 36 spaces in total in the disabled areas,
Lookers Paddock, Seton & Rochdale Road Stands
Helpers: One helper admitted per disabled person
Prices: Free for the disabled. Helpers full price
Disabled Toilets: In Lookers Paddock and Rochdale
Road Stand
Are Bookings Necessary: Yes
Contact: (0161) 624-4972

Travelling Supporters' Information:
Routes: From All Parts: Exit M62 at Junction 20 and take A627M to junction with the A664. Take the 1st exit at roundabout on to Broadway, then 1st right into Hilbre Avenue which leads to the car park.

OXFORD UNITED FC

Founded: 1893 (**Entered League:** 1962)
Former Names: Headington United FC
(1893-1960)
Nickname: 'U's'
Ground: Manor Ground, London Road,
Headington, Oxford   OX3 7RS
Record Attendance: 22,730 (29/2/64)

Colours: Shirts – Yellow with navy sleeves
Shorts – Navy with yellow trim
Telephone Nº: (01865) 61503
Ticket Office: (01865) 61503
Fax Number: (01865) 741820
Pitch Size: 110 × 75 yards
Ground Capacity: 9,572
Seating Capacity: 2,777

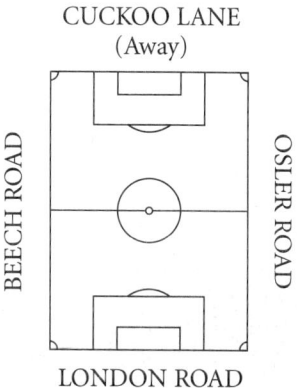

CUCKOO LANE
(Away)

BEECH ROAD

OSLER ROAD

LONDON ROAD

GENERAL INFORMATION

Supporters Club: Gary Whiting, c/o The Club
Telephone Nº: (01865) 63063
Car Parking: Street Parking
Coach Parking: Off Headley Way in Franklin Road
Nearest Railway Station: Oxford (3 miles)
Nearest Bus Station: Queen's Lane (2 miles)
Club Shop: The United Experience, Headington
Opening Times: Wednesday to Friday 12.30–4.00;
Saturdays 11.00am – 1.00pm (Matchdays until 2.45)
Telephone Nº: (01865) 61503
Postal Sales: Yes
Nearest Police Station: Cowley (2 miles)
Police Telephone Nº: (01865) 749909

GROUND INFORMATION

Away Supporters' Entrances & Sections:
Cuckoo Lane turnstiles 5-11 for Cuckoo Lane Stand

ADMISSION INFO (1996/97 PRICES)

Adult Standing: £8.50 – £9.50
Adult Seating: £12.00
Child Standing: £5.50 – £6.00
Child Seating: £8.00
Programme Price: £1.30
Note: Prices vary according to category of match &
Away fans concessions not available on match days

DISABLED INFORMATION

Wheelchairs: 25 spaces in total for Home and Away
fans in the disabled section, Beech Road Corner
Helpers: One helper admitted per disabled person
Prices: £5.00 for disabled. Helpers normal prices
Disabled Toilets: Available in Beech Road corner
Are Bookings Necessary: Yes
Contact: (01865) 61503

Travelling Supporters' Information:
Routes: From North: Exit M40 at Junction 9. Follow signs to Oxford (A34). Take slip road A44 marked Witney, Woodstock. At
roundabout take 1st exit (Pear Tree). Follow to next roundabout A44 junction with A40 Woodstock Road, take 2nd exit marked A40
London. Down to next roundabout (Banbury Road), take 2nd exit to Northern by-pass. Cars take next left turn at slip road marked
New Marston ½ mile and JR Hospital 1 mile. (Coaches follow diversions to avoid weak bridge, next roundabout A40 (Green Road),
take 5th exit, follow signs for A40 junction with B4105 Marston). Down to mini-roundabout and turn left. Straight up Headley
Way, coaches should take 2nd junction right marked Franklin Road (leads to Coach Park). Cars – side street parking only. Take care
for matchday parking restrictions; From South: A34 by-pass to Junction A44 Pear Tree (then as North); From East: Cars and
coaches follow diversion directions a from Green Road roundabout; From West: Take A34 following signs to M40. Take exit A44
marked Woodstock, take 3rd exit (Pear Tree), then as North.

PETERBOROUGH UNITED FC

Founded: 1923 (**Entered League:** 1960) **Former Names:** Peterborough and Fletton United FC (1923-34) **Nickname:** 'Posh' **Ground:** London Road, Peterborough, Cambs. PE2 8AL **Record Attendance:** 30,096 (20/2/65)	**Colours:** Shirts – Blue Shorts – White **Telephone Nº:** (01733) 63947 **Ticket Office:** (01733) 63947 **Fax Number:** (01733) 557210 **Pitch Size:** 112 × 71 yards **Ground Capacity:** 14,856 **Seating Capacity:** 9,576

MOYS END
(Away)

LONDON ROAD

GENERAL INFORMATION

Supporters Club: Ray Duke, c/o Club
Telephone Nº: –
Car Parking: Ample parking at the ground
Coach Parking: At the rear of the ground
Nearest Railway Station: Peterborough (1 mile)
Nearest Bus Station: Peterborough (¼ mile)
Club Shop: At Ground
Opening Times: Monday – Friday 9.00am – 5.00pm
Telephone Nº: (01733) 69760
Postal Sales: Yes
Nearest Police Stat'n: Bridge Street, Peterborough
(5 minutes walk)
Police Telephone Nº: (01733) 63232

GROUND INFORMATION

Away Supporters' Entrances & Sections:
Turnstile A, Moys End for Block A Seating

ADMISSION INFO (1996/97 PRICES)

Adult Standing: £7.00
Adult Seating: £11.00
Child Standing: £3.50 (Home fans only)
Child Seating: £5.50
Programme Price: £1.20

DISABLED INFORMATION

Wheelchairs: 12 spaces in total for Home and Away
fans in the disabled area, right side of Main Stand
Helpers: One helper admitted per disabled person
Prices: £7.00 each for the disabled and helpers
Disabled Toilets: None
Are Bookings Necessary: Yes
Contact: (01733) 63947

Travelling Supporters' Information:
Routes: From North and West: Take A1 then A47 into the Town Centre and follow Whittlesey signs across the river into London Road; From East: Take A47 into the Town Centre (then as North); From South: Take A1 then A15 into London Road.

PLYMOUTH ARGYLE FC

Founded: 1886 (**Entered League:** 1920)	**Telephone Nº:** (01752) 562561
Former Names: Argyle FC (1886-1903)	**Ticket Office:** (01752) 562561
Nickname: 'Pilgrims'; 'Argyle'	**Fax Number:** (01752) 606167
Ground: Home Park, Plymouth PL2 3DQ	**Pitch Size:** 112 × 72 yards
Record Attendance: 43,596 (10/10/36)	**Ground Capacity:** 19,900
Colours: Shirts – Green and Black Stripes	**Seating Capacity:** 6,700
Shorts – Black	

BARN PARK END
(Away)

TAVISTOCK ROAD
LYNDHURST STAND

MAYFLOWER ENCLOSURE
GRAND STAND

DAVENPORT END

GENERAL INFORMATION

Supporters Club: S. Rendell, c/o Club
Telephone Nº: (01752) 562561
Car Parking: Car park for 1,000 cars is adjacent
Coach Parking: Central Car Park
Nearest Railway Station: Plymouth North Road
Nearest Bus Station: Bretonside, Plymouth
Club Shop: At Ground
Opening Times: Monday to Saturday 9.00am – 5.00pm
Telephone Nº: (01752) 558292
Postal Sales: Yes
Nearest Police Station: Devonport (1 mile)
Police Telephone Nº: (01752) 701188

GROUND INFORMATION

Away Supporters' Entrances & Sections:
Barn Park End turnstiles for open accommodation

ADMISSION INFO (1996/97 PRICES)

Adult Standing: £6.50 or £7.00
Adult Seating: £9.00 – £11.00
Child Standing: £3.50, £5.00 or £5.50
Child Seating: £7.00 – £9.00
Programme Price: £1.50
Note: Special rates for adults and children in the Family Enclosure (Prices shown are for category 'A' games – category 'B' and 'C' games will be at a higher price).

DISABLED INFORMATION

Wheelchairs: 60 spaces in total for Home and Away fans in the disabled section, Devonport End
Helpers: One helper admitted per disabled person
Prices: Free of charge for disabled. Helpers £6.50
Disabled Toilets: Adjacent to the disabled section Commentaries are available for the blind
Are Bookings Necessary: Yes
Contact: (01752) 562561

Travelling Supporters' Information:
Routes: From All Parts: Take A38 to Tavistock Road (A386), then branch left following signs for Plymouth (A386) and continue for 1¼ miles. The car park is on the left (signposted Home Park).

PORTSMOUTH FC

Founded: 1898 **(Entered League:** 1920)
Former Names: None
Nickname: 'Pompey'
Ground: Fratton Park, 57 Frogmore Road
Portsmouth, Hants   PO4 8RA
Record Attendance: 51,385 (26/2/49)

Colours: Shirts – Blue
          Shorts – White
Telephone N°: (01705) 731204
Ticket Office: (01705) 750825
Fax Number: (01705) 734129
Pitch Size: 114 × 72 yards
Ground Capacity: 11,200 (All seats)

FROGMORE ROAD
FRATTON END

CARISBROOKE ROAD
SOUTH STAND

MILTON ROAD
NORTH STAND

(Away)
MILTON END
ASPLEY ROAD

GENERAL INFORMATION
Supporters Club: c/o The Club
Telephone N°: –
Car Parking: Street Parking
Coach Parking: By Police direction
Nearest Railway Station: Fratton (adjacent)
Nearest Bus Station: Hilsea
Club Shop: At Ground
Opening Times: Monday – Friday 9.00am – 5.00pm
Saturdays 10.00am – 2.00pm
Telephone N°: (01705) 738358
Postal Sales: Yes
Nearest Police Station: Southsea
Police Telephone N°: (01705) 321111

GROUND INFORMATION
Away Supporters' Entrances & Sections:
Aspley Road – Milton Road side for Aspley Road End

ADMISSION INFO (1996/97 PRICES)
Adult Seating: £10.00 – £15.00
Child Seating: £5.00 – £8.00
Programme Price: £1.50

DISABLED INFORMATION
Wheelchairs: Limited number of spaces available in
the disabled section, Fratton End
Helpers: One helper admitted per disabled person
Prices: Free for the disabled. Helpers pay full price
Disabled Toilets: One available in disabled section
Are Bookings Necessary: Yes
Contact: (01705) 731204

Travelling Supporters' Information:
Routes: From North and West: Take M27 and M275 to the end then take the 2nd exit at the roundabout and after ¼ mile turn right at the 'T' junction into London Road (A2047). After 1¼ miles cross the railway bridge and turn left into Goldsmith Avenue. After ½ mile turn left into Frogmore Road; From East: Take A27 following Southsea signs (A2030). Turn left at the roundabout (3 miles) onto A288, then right into Priory Crescent and next right into Carisbrooke Road.

PORT VALE FC

Founded: 1876 (**Entered League:** 1892)
Former Names: Burslem Port Vale FC
Nickname: 'Valiants'
Ground: Vale Park, Burslem, Stoke-on-Trent ST6 1AW
Record Attendance: 49,768 (20/2/60)
Pitch Size: 114 × 77 yards

Colours: Shirts – White
 Shorts – Black
Telephone Nº: (01782) 814134
Ticket Office: (01782) 814134
Fax Number: (01782) 834981
Ground Capacity: 22,356
Seating Capacity: 17,616

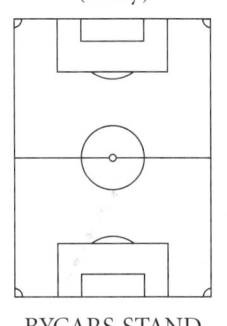

HAMIL ROAD
CAUDWELL STAND
(Away)

LORNE STREET
(Disabled)

RAILWAY STAND

BYCARS STAND

GENERAL INFORMATION

Supporters Club: c/o John Greatbach, Port Vale Supporters' Group, 90 Park Lane, Knypersley, Stoke, ST8 7BQ
Telephone Nº: (01782) 514721
Car Parking: Car parks at the ground
Coach Parking: Hamil Road car park
Nearest Railway Station: Stoke
Nearest Bus Station: Burslem (adjacent)
Club Shop: At Ground
Opening Times: Monday to Saturday 9.00am – 5.30pm
Telephone Nº: (01782) 833545
Postal Sales: Yes
Nearest Police Station: Burslem
Police Telephone Nº: (01782) 577114

GROUND INFORMATION

Away Supporters' Entrances & Sections:
Hamil Road turnstiles for Caudwell Stand

ADMISSION INFO (1996/97 PRICES)

Adult Standing: £9.00 – £9.50
Adult Seating: £11.00 – £12.00
Child Standing: £6.50
Child Seating: £8.00 – £9.00
(Discounts for child concessions when pre-booked)
Programme Price: £1.50

DISABLED INFORMATION

Wheelchairs: 72 spaces in total in the disabled section, Lorne Street/Hamil Road Corner
Helpers: One helper admitted per disabled person
Prices: £5.00 for the disabled. £6.50 for helpers
Disabled Toilets: One available in the disabled area
Commentaries are available – please contact the club for further information
Are Bookings Necessary: Yes
Contact: (01782) 814134

Travelling Supporters' Information:
Routes: From North: Exit M6 at Junction 16 and follow Stoke signs (A500). Branch left off the A500 at the exit signposted Tunstall, take 2nd exit at roundabout into Newcastle Street. Proceed through traffic lights into Moorland Road and take 2nd turning on the left into Hamil Road; From South and West: Exit M6 at Junction 15 and take A5006 and A500. After 6¼ miles branch left (then as North); From East: Take A50 or A52 into Stoke following Burslem signs into Waterloo Road, turn right at Burslem crossroads into Moorland Road (then as North).

PRESTON NORTH END FC

Founded: 1881 **(Entered League:** 1888)
Nickname: 'Lilywhites'; 'North End'
Ground: Deepdale, Preston   PR1 6RU
Record Attendance: 42,684 (23/4/38)
Colours: Shirts – White with Navy Trim
          Shorts – Blue

Telephone Nº: (01772) 902020
Ticket Office: (01772) 902020
Fax Number: (01772) 653266
Pitch Size: 110 × 72 yards
Ground Capacity: 18,700
Seating Capacity: 9,000

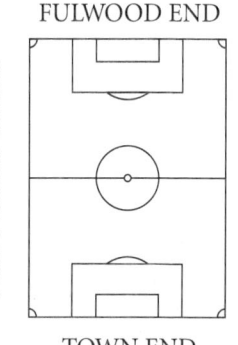

SPION KOP
FULWOOD END

TOM FINNEY STAND

PAVILION STAND (Away)

LOWTHORPE ROAD

TOWN END

GENERAL INFORMATION

Supporters Club: c/o The Club
Telephone Nº: –
Car Parking: West Stand car park (600 cars)
Coach Parking: West Stand car park
Nearest Railway Station: Preston (2 miles)
Nearest Bus Station: Preston (1 mile)
Club Shop: At Ground
Opening Times: Monday to Friday 9.00am –
5.00pm;   Matchdays 12.30pm – 5.00pm
Telephone Nº: (01772) 902040
Postal Sales: Yes
Nearest Police Station: Lawson Street (1 mile)
Police Telephone Nº: (01772) 203203

GROUND INFORMATION

Away Supporters' Entrances & Sections:
Pavilion Stand turnstiles for Pavilion Stand Paddock

ADMISSION INFO (1996/97 PRICES)

Adult Standing: £8.00 – £8.50
Adult Seating: £10.00 – £11.00
Child Standing: £4.50 – £5.00
Child Seating: £6.00 – £7.00
Programme Price: £1.30

DISABLED INFORMATION

Wheelchairs: 100 spaces available in the Tom
Finney Stand
Helpers: One helper admitted per wheelchair
Prices: One disabled person + one helper is free.
Others full price
Disabled Toilets: Available in Tom Finney Stand
Commentaries are available for the blind
Are Bookings Necessary: Usually
Contact: (01772) 902020

Travelling Supporters' Information:
Routes: From North: Take M6 then M55 to Junction 1. Follow signs for Preston A6. After 2 miles turn left at the crossroads into Blackpool Road (A5085). Turn right ¾ mile into Deepdale; From South and East: Exit M6 at Junction 31 and follow Preston signs (A59). Take the 2nd exit at the roundabout (1 mile) into Blackpool Road. Turn left after 1¼ miles into Deepdale; From West: Exit M55 at Junction 1 (then as North).

QUEEN'S PARK RANGERS FC

Founded: 1882 (**Entered League:** 1920)
Former Names: Amalgamation of
St. Jude's FC & Christchurch Rangers FC
Nickname: 'Rangers'; 'R's'
Ground: Rangers Stadium, South Africa
Road, London W12 7PA
Record Attendance: 35,353 (27/4/74)

Colours: Shirts – Blue and White Hoops
Shorts – White
Telephone N°: (0181) 743-0262
Ticket Office: (0181) 740-0503
Fax Number: (0181) 749-0994
Pitch Size: 112 × 72 yards
Ground Capacity: 19,003 (All seats)

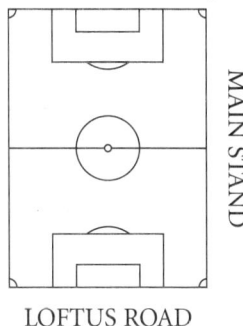

BLOEMFONTEIN ROAD
SCHOOL END (Away)

ELLERSLIE ROAD STAND (Disabled)

SOUTH AFRICA ROAD MAIN STAND

LOFTUS ROAD
STAND

GENERAL INFORMATION

Supporters Club: Patricia Dix, c/o The Club
Telephone N°: (0181) 740-2534
Car Parking: Street Parking
Coach Parking: By Police direction
Nearest Railway Station: Shepherd's Bush
Nearest Tube Station: White City (Central)
Club Shop: At Ground
Opening Times: Monday to Friday 9.30am –
4.45pm; Saturday 9.30am – 12.00pm
Telephone N°: (0181) 749-6862
Postal Sales: Yes
Nearest Police Station: Uxbridge Road, Shepherd's
Bush (½ mile)
Police Telephone N°: (0181) 741-6212

GROUND INFORMATION

Away Supporters' Entrances & Sections:
South Africa Road turnstiles 13-15 & Ellerslie Road
turnstiles 9-12 for School End Stand

ADMISSION INFO (1996/97 PRICES)

Adult Seating: £8.00 – £15.00
Child Seating: £4.00 – £7.50
Programme Price: £1.50
Note: Lower prices are available for members only

DISABLED INFORMATION

Wheelchairs: 18 spaces in the Wheelchair enclosure,
left side of the Ellerslie Road Stand
Helpers: One helper admitted per wheelchair
Prices: Free of charge for Disabled and Helpers
Disabled Toilets: Available in corner of Ellerslie
Road Stand
Commentaries are available for the blind
Are Bookings Necessary: Yes
Contact: Please contact the club in writing

Travelling Supporters' Information:
Routes: From North: Take M1 & M406 North Circular for Neasden, left after ¾ mile (A404) following signs
Harlesden, Hammersmith, past White City Stadium, right into White City Road, left into South Africa Road; From
South: Take A206, A3 across Putney Bridge follow signs to Hammersmith, Oxford A219 to Shepherd's Bush. Join
A4020 following signs to Acton, turn right (¼ mile) into Loftus Road; From East: Take A12, A406 then A503 to join
Ring Road, follow Oxford signs join A40(M), branch left (2 miles) to M41, 3rd exit at roundabout to A4020 (then as
South); From West: Take M4 to Chiswick then A315 & A402 to Shepherd's Bush, join A4020 (then as South).

READING FC

Founded: 1871 (**Entered League:** 1920)
Former Names: Amalgamated with
Hornets FC (1877) and Earley FC (1889)
Nickname: 'Royals'
Ground: Elm Park, Norfolk Road,
Reading   RG3 2EF
Record Attendance: 33,042 (19/2/27)

Colours: Shirts – Blue and White
    Shorts – White
Telephone Nº: (01734) 507878
Ticket Office: (01734) 507878
Fax Number: (01734) 566628
Pitch Size: 112 × 77 yards
Ground Capacity: 14,058
Seating Capacity: 2,242

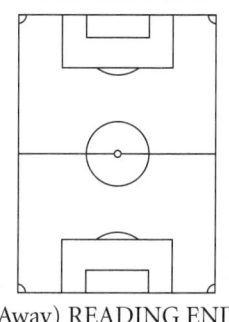

WANTAGE ROAD
TILEHURST END

TILEHURST ROAD (SOUTH BANK)

NORFOLK ROAD

(Away) READING END
SUFFOLK ROAD

GENERAL INFORMATION

Supporters Club: Gerry McGreevy, c/o The Club
Telephone Nº: (01734) 507878
Car Parking: Street parking/Prospect School/Park and Ride
Coach Parking: By Police direction
Nearest Railway Station: Reading West (½ mile), Reading General (2½ miles)
Nearest Bus Station: Reading
Club Shop: Via Ticket Office
Opening Times: Monday to Friday and Matchdays 9.00am – 5.00pm
Telephone Nº; (01734) 507878
Postal Sales: /Yes
Nearest Police Stat'n: Castle Street, Reading (2 mls)
Police Telephone Nº: (01734) 536000

GROUND INFORMATION

Away Supporters' Entrances & Sections:
Norfolk Road turnstiles 23-29 for Reading End

ADMISSION INFO (1996/97 PRICES)

Adult Standing: £8.00
Adult Seating: £9.00 – £12.00
Child Standing: £5.00
Child Seating: Concessions in Family Stand only
Programme Price: £1.50

DISABLED INFORMATION

Wheelchairs: 16 spaces in total for Home and Away fans in the disabled area, in Front Row of 'E' Stand
Helpers: Yes
Prices: £5.00 for each disabled person + one helper
Disabled Toilets: One available adjacent to stand
Are Bookings Necessary: Yes
Contact: (01734) 566628

Travelling Supporters' Information:
Routes: From North: Take A423, A4074 and A4155 from Oxford across the railway bridge into Reading. Follow signs for Newbury (A4) into Castle Hill, then right into Tilehurst Road. Turn right after ¾ mile into Cranbury Road then left and 2nd left into Norfolk Road; From South: Take A33 into Reading and follow Newbury signs into Bath Road. Cross railway bridge and take 3rd exit into Liebenrood Road. At the end turn right into Tilehurst Road then 1st left into Cranbury Road and 2nd left into Norfolk Road; From East and West: Exit M4 at Junction 12 and take A4. After 3¼ miles turn left into Liebenrood Road (then as South).

ROCHDALE FC

Founded: 1907 (**Entered League:** 1921)
Former Names: Rochdale Town FC
Nickname: 'The Dale'
Ground: Willbutts Lane, Spotland,
Rochdale   OL11 5DS
Record Attendance: 24,231 (10/12/49)
Pitch Size: 114 × 76 yards

Colours: Shirts – Blue and White
Shorts – Blue
Telephone Nº: (01706) 44648
Ticket Office: (01706) 44648
Fax Number: (01706) 48466
Ground Capacity: 6,448
Seating Capacity: 1,852

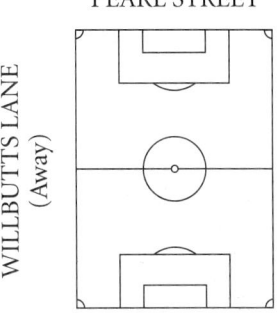

PEARL STREET

WILLBUTTS LANE (Away)

MAIN STAND

SANDY LANE STAND

GENERAL INFORMATION

Supporters Club: F. Duffy, c/o The Club
Telephone Nº: (01706) 852498
Car Parking: Street Parking
Coach Parking: By Police direction
Nearest Railway Station: Rochdale (2 miles)
Nearest Bus Station: Town Centre (1 mile)
Club Shop: At Ground
Opening Times: Weekdays 9.15am – 5.30pm and
Matchdays 9.15am – 6.00pm
Telephone Nº: (01706) 47521
Postal Sales: Yes
Nearest Police Station: Rochdale (1½ miles)
Police Telephone Nº: (01706) 47401

GROUND INFORMATION

Away Supporters' Entrances & Sections:
Turnstiles 16, 17 and 18 for Willbutts Lane

ADMISSION INFO (1996/97 PRICES)

Adult Standing: £7.00
Adult Seating: £9.00
Child Standing: £4.00
Child Seating: £5.00
Additional child concessions available in Family
Section of Main Stand only. Above prices are for
category 'A' games and may be higher for certain
fixtures during the 1996/97 game
Programme Price: £1.50

DISABLED INFORMATION

Wheelchairs: 12 spaces in total for Home and Away
fans in the disabled section, Main Stand
Helpers: One helper admitted per disabled person
Prices: Free of charge for disabled. Helpers £9.00
Disabled Toilets: Available adjacent to disabled area
Are Bookings Necessary: Yes
Contact: (01706) 44648

Travelling Supporters' Information:
Routes: From All Parts: Exit M62 at Junction 20 following signs for Rochdale. After 1½ miles take the 2nd exit at the 2nd roundabout into Roch Valley Way signposted Blackburn. At the next traffic lights go straight ahead and the ground is on the right after ½ mile.

ROTHERHAM UNITED FC

Founded: 1884 (**Entered League:** 1893)	**Colours:** Shirts – Red
Former Names: Thornhill United FC	Shorts – White
(1884-1905); Rotherham County FC	**Telephone N°:** (01709) 512434
(1905-1925)	**Ticket Office:** (01709) 512434
Nickname: 'The Merry Millers'	**Fax Number:** (01709) 512762
Ground: Millmoor Ground, Rotherham,	**Pitch Size:** 115 × 76 yards
S60 1HR	**Ground Capacity:** 11,533
Record Attendance: 25,000 (13/12/52)	**Seating Capacity:** 3,407

RAILWAY END
(Away)

MILLMOOR LANE STAND (Away)

MAIN STAND

TIVOLI END
MASBOROUGH STREET

GENERAL INFORMATION

Supporters Club: c/o Mrs R. Cowley, 50 Lister Street, Rotherham
Telephone N°: (01709) 375831
Car Parking: Kimberworth Road and Main Street car parks
Coach Parking: By Police direction
Nearest Railway Station: Rotherham Central (½ m)
Nearest Bus Station: Town Centre (½ mile)
Club Shop: At Ground
Opening Times: Weekdays 9.00am – 5.00pm
Telephone N°: (01709) 512760
Postal Sales: Yes
Nearest Police Station: Rotherham (½ mile)
Police Telephone N°: (01709) 371121

GROUND INFORMATION

Away Supporters' Entrances & Sections:
Millmoor Lane turnstiles for Millmoor Lane/Railway End

ADMISSION INFO (1996/97 PRICES)

Adult Standing: £7.50
Adult Seating: £8.50 – £10.00
Child Standing: £5.00
Child Seating: £5.50 – £6.50
Family Stand: Adults £8.00 + £1.00 for 1st child & £5.50 each for others
Programme Price: £1.40

DISABLED INFORMATION

Wheelchairs: 13 spaces in total for Home and Away fans in the disabled section, Millmoor Lane
Helpers: One helper admitted per disabled person
Prices: Disabled and helpers £5.00 each
Disabled Toilets: One available in the disabled area
Are Bookings Necessary: Yes
Contact: (01709) 512434

Travelling Supporters' Information:
Routes: From North: Exit M1 at Junction 34 following Rotherham (A6109) signs to traffic lights and turn right. Ground is ¼ mile on right over railway bridge; From South & West: Exit M1 at Junction 33, turn right following Rotherham signs. Left at roundabout and right at next roundabout. Follow dual carriageway to next roundabout and go straight on. Turn left at next roundabout – ground is ¼ mile on left; From East: Take A630 into Rotherham following Sheffield signs. At 2nd roundabout turn right into Masborough Street then left into Millmoor Lane.

SCARBOROUGH FC

Founded: 1879 (**Entered League:** 1987)	**Colours:** Shirts – Red
Former Names: None	Shorts – White
Nickname: 'Boro'	**Telephone Nº:** (01723) 375094
Ground: McCain Stadium, Seamer Road,	**Ticket Office:** (01723) 375094
Scarborough, N. Yorks YO12 4HF	**Fax Number:** (01723) 378733
Record Attendance: 11,124 (1938)	**Ground Capacity:** 6,899
Pitch Size: 112 × 74 yards	**Seating Capacity:** 3,500

WEST STAND
(Away)

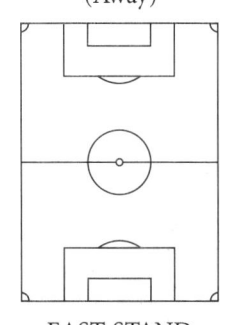

EAST STAND
SEAMER ROAD

GENERAL INFORMATION
Supporters Club: Mrs S. Nettleton, c/o The Club
Telephone Nº: (01723) 375094
Car Parking: Street Parking
Coach Parking: Scarborough Coach Park
Nearest Railway Station: Scarborough Central
(2 miles)
Nearest Bus Station: Westwood Scarborough
(2 miles)
Club Shop: At Ground
Opening Times: Weekdays 9.30am – 5.00pm and
Matchdays
Telephone Nº: (01723) 375094
Postal Sales: Yes
Nearest Police Station: Scarborough (2 miles)
Police Telephone Nº: (01723) 500300

GROUND INFORMATION
Away Supporters' Entrances & Sections:
West Stand turnstiles for West Stand enclosure

ADMISSION INFO (1996/97 PRICES)
Adult Standing: £6.00
Adult Seating: £8.50
Child Standing: £3.50
Child Seating: £6.00
Programme Price: £1.00

DISABLED INFORMATION
Wheelchairs: 20 spaces in total in the Main Stand,
West Stand and East Stand
Helpers: One helper admitted per wheelchair
Prices: Full-price for the disabled and helpers
Disabled Toilets: Available at rear of disabled area
Are Bookings Necessary: Yes
Contact: (01723) 375094

Travelling Supporters' Information:
Routes: The ground is situated on the main York to Scarborough Road (A64), ½ mile on the left past the B&Q
DIY store.

SCUNTHORPE UNITED FC

Founded: 1899 **(Entered League:** 1950)
Former Names: Scunthorpe and Lindsey
United (1899-1912)
Nickname: 'Irons'
Ground: Glanford Park, Doncaster Road,
Scunthorpe, North Lincs.   DN15 8TD
Record Attendance: 8,775 (1/5/89)

Colours: Shirts – White with claret/blue
Shorts – Sky blue + claret/blue
Telephone Nº: (01724) 848077
Ticket Office: (01724) 848077
Fax Number: (01724) 857986
Pitch Size: 111 × 73 yards
Ground Capacity: 9,200
Seating Capacity: 6,400

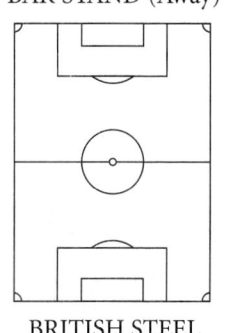

CAPARO MERCHANT
BAR STAND (Away)

CLUGSTON STAND (Disabled)

SCUNTHORPE EVENING TELEGRAPH STAND

BRITISH STEEL
STAND

GENERAL INFORMATION

Supporters Club: c/o A. Webster, 12 Byfield Road,
Scunthorpe
Telephone Nº: (01724) 863009
Car Parking: Spaces for 600 cars at the ground
Coach Parking: At the ground
Nearest Railway Station: Scunthorpe (1½ miles)
Nearest Bus Station: Scunthorpe (1½ miles)
Club Shop: At the ground
Opening Times: Weekdays 9.00am – 5.00pm
Matchdays 10.30am – 3.00pm & 4.45pm – 5.15pm
Telephone Nº: (01724) 848077
Postal Sales: Yes
Nearest Police Station: Laneham Street,
Scunthorpe (1½ miles)
Police Telephone Nº: (01724) 282888

GROUND INFORMATION

Away Supporters' Entrances & Sections:
Turnstiles 6-7 for the Caparo Merchant Bar Stand

ADMISSION INFO (1996/97 PRICES)

Adult Standing: £6.50
Adult Seating: £8.00 – £9.00
Child Standing: £3.30
Child Seating: £4.00 or £5.50
Additional child concessions are available when
purchased in advance
Programme Price: £1.50

DISABLED INFORMATION

Wheelchairs: 12 spaces each for Home and Away
fans in the disabled section, Clugston Stand
Helpers: One helper admitted per disabled person
Prices: Free for the disabled. Helpers full-price
Disabled Toilets: One available in the disabled area
Commentaries are available for the blind
Are Bookings Necessary: Yes
Contact: (01724) 848077

Travelling Supporters' Information:
Routes: From All Parts: Exit M180 at Junction 3 onto M181. Follow M181 to roundabout with A18 and take A18
towards Scunthorpe – the ground is on the right 200 yards from the roundabout.

SHEFFIELD UNITED FC

Founded: 1889 (**Entered League:** 1892)	**Colours:** Shirts – Red and White Stripes
Former Names: None	Shorts – Black
Nickname: 'Blades'	**Telephone Nº:** (0114) 273-8955
Ground: Bramall Lane, Sheffield S2 4SU	**Ticket Office:** (0114) 276-6771
Record Attendance: 68,287 (15/2/36)	**Fax Number:** (0114) 272-3030
	Pitch Size: 112 × 72 yards
	Ground Capacity: 30,000 (All seats)

SHOREHAM STREET
KOP SEATS

JOHN STREET STAND

CHERRY STREET
LAVER STAND

LOWER (Home)
UPPER (Away)
BRAMALL LANE

GENERAL INFORMATION

Supporters Club: c/o Beryl Whitney, 42 Base Green Avenue, Sheffield S12 3FA
Telephone Nº: (0114) 239-0202
Car Parking: Street Parking
Coach Parking: By Police direction
Nearest Railway Station: Sheffield Midland (1 mile)
Nearest Bus Station: Pond Street, Sheffield
Club Shop: At Ground
Opening Times: Monday to Friday 9.30am – 5.00pm & Matchdays 9.30am – 5.30pm
Telephone Nº: (0114) 275-0596
Postal Sales: Yes
Nearest Police Station: Police Room at the ground
Police Telephone Nº: (0114) 276-8522

GROUND INFORMATION

Away Supporters' Entrances & Sections:
Bramall Lane turnstiles – Bramall Lane Upper Stand

ADMISSION INFO (1996/97 PRICES)

Adult Seating: £10.00 – £16.00
Child Seating: £5.00 – £8.00
Programme Price: £1.50

DISABLED INFORMATION

Wheelchairs: Limited number of spaces available in the disabled section – Members area
Helpers: One helper admitted per wheelchair
Prices: Contact the club for further details
Disabled Toilets: 3 available within the enclosure
Commentaries available for the blind on request
Are Bookings Necessary: Yes
Contact: (0114) 273-8955

Travelling Supporters' Information:
Routes: From North: Exit M1 at Junction 34 following signs to Sheffield (A6109), turn left after 3½ miles and take 4th exit at the roundabout into Sheaf Street. Take the 5th exit at the 2nd roundabout into St. Mary's Road (for Bakewell), turn left ½ mile into Bramall Lane; From South and East: Exit M1 at Junctions 31 or 33 and take A57 to the roundabout, take the 3rd exit into Sheaf Street (then as North); From West: Take A57 into Sheffield and take 4th exit at roundabout into Upper Hanover Street and at 2nd roundabout take 3rd exit into Bramall Lane.

SHEFFIELD WEDNESDAY FC

<table>
<tr><td>

Founded: 1867 (**Entered League:** 1892)
Former Names: The Wednesday FC
Nickname: 'Owls'
Ground: Hillsborough, Sheffield S6 1SW
Record Attendance: 72,841 (17/2/34)

</td><td>

Colours: Shirts – Blue and White Stripes
    Shorts – Black
Telephone N°: (0114) 234-3122
Ticket Office: (0114) 233-7233
Fax Number: (0114) 233-7145
Pitch Size: 115 × 75 yards
Ground Capacity: 36,020 (All seats)

</td></tr>
</table>

PENISTONE ROAD
KOP STAND

NORTH STAND

RIVER DON
SOUTH STAND

(Away)
WEST STAND

GENERAL INFORMATION

Supporters Club: –
Telephone N°: –
Car Parking: Street Parking
Coach Parking: Owlerton Stadium
Nearest Railway Station: Sheffield Midland (4 mls)
Nearest Bus Station: Pond Street, Sheffield (4 miles)
Club Shop: At Ground
Opening Times: Monday to Saturday 10.00am – 4.30pm
Telephone N°: (0114) 234-3342
Postal Sales: Yes
Nearest Police Station: Hammerton Road, Sheffield (1 mile)
Police Telephone N°: (0114) 234-3131

GROUND INFORMATION

Away Supporters' Entrances & Sections:
West Stand turnstiles for West Stand, Lower Tier

ADMISSION INFO (1996/97 PRICES)

Adult Seating: £8.00 – £18.00
Child Seating: £4.50 – £12.00
Programme Price: £1.50
Note: Prices vary depending on category of game

DISABLED INFORMATION

Wheelchairs: Unspecified number of spaces in the disabled section – North Stand
Helpers: One helper admitted per disabled person
Prices: Normal prices for the disabled and helpers
Disabled Toilets: Available within the North Stand Commentaries are available for the blind
Are Bookings Necessary: Yes
Contact: (0114) 234-3122

Travelling Supporters' Information:
Routes: From North: Exit M1 at Junction 34 following signs for Sheffield (A6109), after 1½ miles take the 3rd exit at the roundabout and after 3¼ miles turn left into Herries Road for the ground; From South and East: Exit M1 at Junctions 31 or 33 and take A57 to the roundabout and take the exit into Prince of Wales Road. After 5¾ miles turn left into Herries Road South; From West: Take A57 until A6101 and turn left. After 3¾ miles turn left at the 'T' junction into Penistone Road for the ground.

SHREWSBURY TOWN FC

Founded: 1886 (**Entered League:** 1950)
Former Names: None
Nickname: 'Town'
Ground: Gay Meadow, Shrewsbury,
SY2 6AB
Record Attendance: 18,917 (26/4/61)
Pitch Size: 116 × 75 yards

Colours: Shirts – Blue with White Trim
Shorts – Blue with White Trim
Telephone Nº: (01743) 360111
Ticket Office: (01743) 360111
Fax Number: (01743) 236384
Ground Capacity: 8,000
Seating Capacity: 3,000

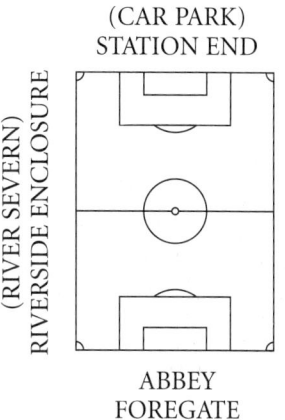

(CAR PARK)
STATION END
STATION STAND
(RIVER SEVERN) RIVERSIDE ENCLOSURE
CENTRE STAND
WAKEMAN STAND
ABBEY FOREGATE

GENERAL INFORMATION

Supporters Club: Peter Sandford, c/o The Club
Telephone Nº: (01743) 360111
Car Parking: Car park adjacent to the ground
Coach Parking: Gay Meadow
Nearest Railway Station: Shrewsbury (1 mile)
Nearest Bus Station: Baker Street, Shrewsbury
Club Shop: At Ground
Opening Times: Matchdays and Office Hours
Telephone Nº: (01743) 356316
Postal Sales: Yes
Nearest Police Station: Clive Road, Shrewsbury
Police Telephone Nº: (01743) 232888

GROUND INFORMATION

Away Supporters' Entrances & Sections:
Station End turnstiles for Station Stand (covered)

ADMISSION INFO (1996/97 PRICES)

Adult Standing: £7.00
Adult Seating: £9.00 – £10.00 (Members only)
Child Standing: £4.00 (Members only)
Child Seating: £5.00 (Wakeman Stand)
Away Standing: £7.00 (No concessions)
Away Seating: £10.00 (No concessions)
Programme Price: £1.30

DISABLED INFORMATION

Wheelchairs: 4 spaces each for home fans and away
fans in two areas at the side of the stands
Helpers: One helper admitted per disabled person
Prices: Free for the disabled. Full-price for helpers
Disabled Toilets: One available in Wakeman Stand
Are Bookings Necessary: Yes
Contact: (01743) 360111

Travelling Supporters' Information:
Routes: From North: Take A49 or A53 then 2nd exit at the roundabout into Telford Way (A5112). After ¾ mile take 2nd exit at the roundabout. Turn right at 'T' junction into Abbey Foregate for the ground; From South: Take A49 to the Town Centre and at the end of Coleham Head turn right into Abbey Foregate; From East: Take A5 then A458 into the Town Centre and go straight forward into Abbey Foregate; From West: Take A458 then A5 around Ring Road to Roman Road, then turn left into Hereford Road and at the end of Coleman Head turn right into Abbey Forecourt.

SOUTHAMPTON FC

Founded: 1885 (**Entered League:** 1920) **Former Names:** Southampton St. Mary's YMCA FC (1885-1897) **Nickname:** 'Saints' **Ground:** The Dell, Milton Road, Southampton SO15 2XH **Record Attendance:** 31,044 (8/10/69)	**Colours:** Shirts – Red and White Shorts – Black **Telephone Nº:** (01703) 220505 **Ticket Office:** (01703) 220505 **Fax Number:** (01703) 330360 **Pitch Size:** 110 × 72 yards **Ground Capacity:** 15,000 (All seats)

WILTON AVENUE
MILTON ROAD

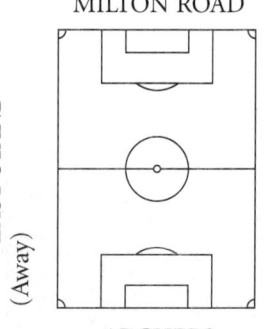

EAST STAND
(Away)

HILL LANE/MILTON ROAD
WEST STAND

ARCHERS
ROAD END

GENERAL INFORMATION

Supporters Club: c/o The Secretary, Saints Supporters' Social Club, The Dell, Milton Road, Southampton
Telephone Nº: (01703) 336540
Car Parking: Street Parking
Coach Parking: By Police direction
Nearest Railway Stat'n: Southampton Central (1ml)
Nearest Bus Station: West Quay Road by Centre 2000
Club Shop: At Ground
Opening Times: Monday to Saturday 9.00am – 5.00pm (closed Wednesday)
Telephone Nº: (01703) 236400
Postal Sales: Yes
Nearest Police Station: Civic Centre, Southampton (1 mile)
Police Telephone Nº: (01703) 581111

GROUND INFORMATION

Away Supporters' Entrances & Sections:
Archers Road turnstiles 16-20 for Upper/Lower East Stand Archers Road End

ADMISSION INFO (1996/97 PRICES)

Adult Seating: £14.00 – £16.00
Child Seating: £6.00 – Lower East/West Stand
Programme Price: £1.50

DISABLED INFORMATION

Wheelchairs: 18 spaces in total for Home and Away fans in the disabled section, under the West Stand
Helpers: One helper admitted per disabled person
Prices: Free of charge for disabled. Helpers £10.00
Disabled Toilets: Available by the disabled entrance Commentaries are available for the blind
Are Bookings Necessary: Yes
Contact: (01703) 667547 (Mr. Mortimer)

Travelling Supporters' Information:
Routes: From North: Take A33 into the Avenue and turn right into Northlands Road. Turn right at the end into Archer's Road; From East: Take M27 to A334 and follow signs Southampton A3024. Follow signs for The West into Commercial Road, turn right into Hill Lane then 1st right into Milton Road; From West: Take A35 then A3024 following signs for City Centre into Fourposts Hill then left into Hill Lane and 1st right into Milton Road.

SOUTHEND UNITED FC

Founded: 1906 (**Entered League:** 1920)	**Colours:** Shirts – Blue and Red
Former Names: Southend Athletic FC	Shorts – Blue and Red
Nickname: 'Shrimpers'; 'Blues'	**Telephone Nº:** (01702) 304050
Ground: Roots Hall Ground, Victoria	**Ticket Office:** (01702) 304090
Avenue, Southend-on-Sea SS2 6NQ	**Fax Number:** (01702) 330164
Record Attendance: 31,033 (10/1/79)	**Ground Capacity:** 12,485 (All seats)
Pitch Size: 110 × 74 yards	

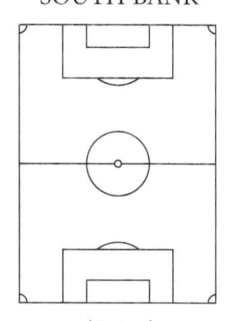

SOUTH BANK

VICTORIA AVENUE
EAST STAND

WEST STAND
SHAKESPEARE DRIVE

(Away)
NORTH STAND
FAIRFAX DRIVE

GENERAL INFORMATION

Supporters Club: Tony Walters, c/o The Club
Telephone Nº: (01702) 304050
Car Parking: Car park at the ground for 500 cars –
Season Ticket holders only + Street parking
Coach Parking: Car park at the ground
Nearest Railway Station: Prittlewell (½ mile)
Nearest Bus Station: London Road, Southend
Club Shop: At the ground and in Town
Opening Times: Ground: Weekdays & Matchdays
10.00am – 5.00pm (except Wednesdays); Town:
Monday to Saturday 9.30am – 5.00pm
Telephone Nº: (01702) 304140 (Ground);
(01702) 801351 (Town)
Postal Sales: Yes
Nearest Police Station: Southend-on-Sea (¼ mile)
Police Telephone Nº: (01702) 431212

GROUND INFORMATION

Away Supporters' Entrances & Sections:
North Stand turnstiles for North Stand seating

ADMISSION INFO (1996/97 PRICES)

Adult Seating: £8.00 – £15.00
Child Seating: £4.00 – £6.00
Away Seating: £12.00 (purchased on matchday)
Programme Price: £1.50

DISABLED INFORMATION

Wheelchairs: 20 spaces in total for Home and Away
fans in the disabled section, West Stand
Helpers: One helper admitted per disabled person
Prices: £5.00 or £6.00 per wheelchair. £10.00 –
£12.00 per adult helper
Disabled Toilets: One available in the disabled area
Commentaries are available for the blind
Are Bookings Necessary: Yes
Contact: (01702) 304090

Travelling Supporters' Information:
Routes: From North and West: Take A127 to Southend then at the roundabout, take the 3rd exit into Victoria
Avenue; From South: Take A13 following signs for Southend then turn left into West Road. At the end of West
Road turn left into Victoria Avenue.

STOCKPORT COUNTY FC

Founded: 1883 (**Entered League:** 1900)
Former Names: Heaton Norris Rovers FC
and Heaton Norris FC
Nickname: 'Hatters'; 'County'
Ground: Edgeley Park, Hardcastle Road,
Edgeley, Stockport   SK3 9DD
Record Attendance: 27,833 (11/2/50)

Colours: Shirts – Blue with red/blue trim
    Shorts – White
Telephone Nº: (0161) 286-8888
Ticket Office: (0161) 286-8888
Fax Number: (0161) 286-8900
Pitch Size: 111 × 72 yards
Ground Capacity: Approximately 12,086
Seating Capacity: 12,086

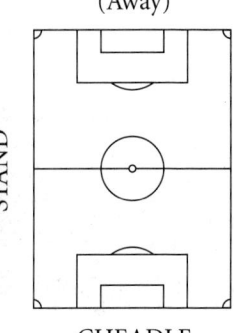

RAILWAY END
(Away)

HARDCASTLE ROAD STAND

VERNON BUILDING SOCIETY STAND

CHEADLE
STAND

GENERAL INFORMATION
Supporters Club: Ken Boxshall, c/o Club Shop
Telephone Nº: (0161) 286-8899
Car Parking: Street Parking
Coach Parking: By Police direction
Nearest Railway Station: Stockport (5 mins. walk)
Nearest Bus Station: Mersey Square (10 mins. walk)
Club Shop: At Ground
Opening Times: Weekdays 9.00am – 5.00pm and
Saturdays 9.30am – 12.30pm
Telephone Nº: (0161) 286-8899
Postal Sales: Yes
Nearest Police Station: Stockport (1 mile)
Police Telephone Nº: (0161) 872-5050

GROUND INFORMATION
Away Supporters' Entrances & Sections:
Railway End turnstiles for Railway End

ADMISSION INFO (1996/97 PRICES)
Adult Seating: £9.00 – £10.00
Child Seating: £4.00
Away Fans: All standing £8.00 (No concessions)
Programme Price: £1.50

DISABLED INFORMATION
Wheelchairs: 10 spaces in total accommodated in
the disabled section, Hardcastle Road Stand
Helpers: One helper admitted per disabled person
Prices: Free for the disabled. Full-price for helpers
Disabled Toilets: None
Are Bookings Necessary: Yes
Contact: (0161) 480-8888

Travelling Supporters' Information:
Routes: From North, South and West: Exit M63 at Junction 11 and join A560, following signs for Cheadle, after
¼ mile turn right into Edgeley Road and after 1 mile turn right into Caroline Street for the ground; From East:
Take A6 or A560 into Stockport Town Centre and turn left into Greek Street. Take 2nd exit into Mercian Way
(from roundabout) then turn left into Caroline Street – the ground is straight ahead.

STOKE CITY FC

Founded: 1863 (**Entered League:** 1888)	**Colours:** Shirts – Red and White Stripes
Former Names: Stoke FC	Shorts – White
Nickname: 'Potters'	**Telephone Nº:** (01782) 413511
Ground: Victoria Ground, Boothen Old	**Ticket Office:** (01782) 413961
Road, Stoke-on-Trent ST4 4EG	**Fax Number:** (01782) 46422
Record Attendance: 51,380 (29/3/37)	**Ground Capacity:** 24,071
Pitch Size: 116 × 72 yards	**Seating Capacity:** 8,494

LONSDALE STREET
STOKE END

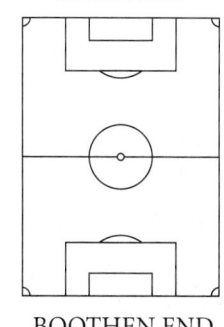

BOOTHEN END

GENERAL INFORMATION

Supporters Club: c/o Nic Mansfield, 11A Westland Street, Penkhull, Stoke-on-Trent   ST4 7HE
Telephone Nº: (01782) 744674
Car Parking: Car park at ground for 2,000 cars
Coach Parking: Whieldon Road
Nearest Railway Station: Stoke-on-Trent (10 mins.)
Nearest Bus Station: Hanley (2 miles)
Club Shop: At Ground
Opening Times: Monday to Friday 9.30am – 5.00pm and Saturdays 9.30am – 12.00pm
Telephone Nº: (01782) 747078
Postal Sales: Yes
Nearest Police Station: Stoke-on-Trent (¼ mile)
Police Telephone Nº: (01782) 744644

GROUND INFORMATION

Away Supporters' Entrances & Sections:
Butler Street turnstiles 47-49 and Stoke End turnstiles 33-35/41-46 for Butler Street Stand Blocks A and B and Stoke End Paddock

ADMISSION INFO (1996/97 PRICES)

Adult Standing: £9.00
Adult Seating: £13.00
Child Standing: £6.00
Child Seating: £7.00
Programme Price: £1.50

DISABLED INFORMATION

Wheelchairs: 25 spaces in total in the disabled section, corner of Butler Street and Boothen End
Helpers: One helper admitted per disabled person
Prices: Free for the disabled. Adult helpers £9.00, Concessionary helpers £7.00
Disabled Toilets: None
15 places are available for commentaries – phone for details
Are Bookings Necessary: Yes
Contact: (01782) 413511

Travelling Supporters' Information:
Routes: From North, South and West: Exit M6 at Junction 15 and follow signs for Stoke (A5006) and join A500. Branch left after ¾ mile and take 2nd exit at the roundabout into Campbell Road for the ground; From East: Take A50 into Stoke Town Centre and turn left at the crossroads into Lonsdale Street for Campbell Road.

SUNDERLAND FC

Founded: 1879 (**Entered League:** 1890)
Former Names: Sunderland and District
Teachers FC
Nickname: 'Rokerites'
Ground: Roker Park, Grantham Road,
Roker, Sunderland   SR6 9SW
Record Attendance: 75,118 (8/3/33)

Colours: Shirts – Red and White Stripes
Shorts – Black
Telephone Nº: (0191) 514-0332
Ticket Office: (0191) 564-2596
Fax Number: (0191) 514-5854
Pitch Size: 113 × 74 yards
Ground Capacity: 22,657
Seating Capacity: 7,753

ROKER BATHS ROAD
(Away) ROKER END

FULLWELL END
HAMPDEN ROAD

ROKER WING · MAIN STAND · FULLWELL WING · ASSOCIATION ROAD CLOCK STAND

GENERAL INFORMATION

Supporters Club: c/o Audrey Baillie, 36 Roker Baths
Road, Roker, Sunderland
Telephone Nº: (0191) 567-0067
Car Parking: Car park for 130 cars & street parking
Coach Parking: Seafront, Roker
Nearest Railway Station: Seaburn
Nearest Bus Station: Town Centre (2 miles)
Club Shop: Town Centre and Roker Park
Opening Times: Monday to Saturday 9.00am –
5.00pm
Telephone Nº: (0191) 564-0002
Postal Sales: Yes
Nearest Police Station: Southwick (1¼ miles)
Police Telephone Nº: (0191) 510-2020

GROUND INFORMATION

Away Supporters' Entrances & Sections:
Roker End turnstiles for Roker End

ADMISSION INFO (1995/96 PRICES)

Adult Standing: £10 Members   £11 Non-members
Adult Seating: £13.00 – £15.00
Child Standing: £6.00
Child Seating: £13.00 (Family Enclosure £9.00)
Note: It is likely that admission will be restricted to
season ticket holders in 1996/97
Programme Price: £1.50

DISABLED INFORMATION

Wheelchairs: 22 spaces for Home fans, 1 for away
fans in the disabled section, Roker Stand
Helpers: One helper admitted per disabled person
Prices: Free of charge for Disabled and Helpers
Disabled Toilets: Available in Roker & Fulwell Ends
Headphone commentaries available in Disabled
section (Main Stand)
Are Bookings Necessary: Yes
Contact: (0191) 514-0332

Travelling Supporters' Information:
Routes: From All Parts: Take A19 to Sunderland. Take A1231 turn-off for Sunderland North and follow the
signs to the City Centre. After 2 miles, at the traffic lights, go straight ahead in the left lane marked A1289 to
Roker. After 1 mile, follow the Roker A183 signs. After 200 yards follow signs for Whitburn and Sea Front (A183)
and after ½ mile turn left down the side street. The football ground is straight ahead.

SWANSEA CITY FC

Founded: 1900 (**Entered League:** 1920)
Former Names: Swansea Town FC (1900-1970)
Nickname: 'Swans'
Ground: Vetch Field, Swansea   SA1 3SU
Record Attendance: 32,796 (17/2/68)
Pitch Size: 110 × 74 yards

Colours: Shirts – White with black sleeves
    Shorts – White + red/black trim
Telephone Nº: (01792) 474114
Ticket Office: (01792) 474114
Fax Number: (01792) 646120
Ground Capacity: 16,499
Seating Capacity: 3,414

WILLIAM STREET
EAST STAND

MADOC STREET
NORTH BANK

GLAMORGAN STREET
CENTRE STAND

(Away)
WEST TERRACE
RICHARDSON STREET

GENERAL INFORMATION

Supporters Club: c/o John Button, 159 Western Street, Swansea
Telephone Nº: (01792) 460958
Car Parking: Kingsway (200 yards) and Clarence Terrace (50 yards) Car Parks + street parking
Coach Parking: By Police direction
Nearest Railway Station: Swansea High Street (1ml)
Nearest Bus Station: Quadrant Depot (¼ mile)
Club Shop: 33 William Street, Swansea   SA1 3QS
Opening Times: Weekdays 10.00am – 4.30pm and Matchdays 9.30am – 5.00pm
Telephone Nº: (01792) 462584
Postal Sales: Yes
Nearest Police Station: Swansea Central (1 mile)
Police Telephone Nº: (01792) 456999

GROUND INFORMATION

Away Supporters' Entrances & Sections:
Richardson Street turnstiles for the West Terrace Enclosure (partially covered)

ADMISSION INFO (1996/97 PRICES)

Adult Standing: £6.50
Adult Seating: £8.50 – £10.00
Child Standing: £3.50
Child Seating: Adult + 1 child = £12.50   Adult + 2 children = £14.50
Programme Price: £1.30

DISABLED INFORMATION

Wheelchairs: 10 spaces in total for Home and Away fans in the disabled section, Centre Stand touchline
Helpers: One helper admitted per wheelchair
Prices: Free of charge for Disabled and Helpers
Disabled Toilets: None
Are Bookings Necessary: Yes
Contact: (01792) 474114

Travelling Supporters' Information:
Routes: From All Parts: Exit M4 at Junction 42 and follow Swansea (A483) signs. After 4 miles follow signs for City Centre West. After ½ turn right (opposite County Hall) into West Way. At first set of traffic lights, turn left into Glamorgan Street from Vetch Field.

SWINDON TOWN FC

Founded: 1881 (**Entered League:** 1920)	**Colours:** Shirts – Red
Former Names: None	Shorts – Red
Nickname: 'Robins'	**Telephone Nº:** (01793) 430430
Ground: County Ground, County Road,	**Ticket Office:** (01793) 529000
Swindon SN1 2ED	**Fax Number:** (01793) 536170
Record Attendance: 32,000 (15/1/72)	**Ground Capacity:** 15,341 (All seats)
Pitch Size: 114 × 74 yards	

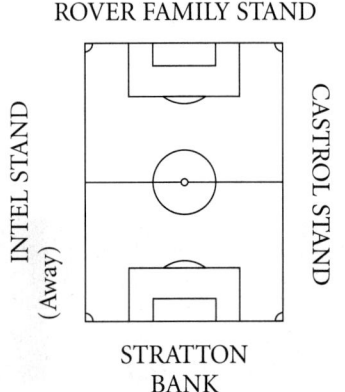

GENERAL INFORMATION

Supporters Club: c/o Miss S. Cobern, 31 Pewsham Road, Penhill, Swindon
Telephone Nº: (01793) 481061
Car Parking: Town Centre
Coach Parking: Car park adjacent to the ground
Nearest Railway Station: Swindon (½ mile)
Nearest Bus Station: Swindon (½ mile)
Club Shop: The Swindon Town Superstore
Opening Times: Weekdays 9.00am – 5.00pm and Saturdays 9.00am – 3.00pm on matchdays only
Telephone Nº: (01793) 423030
Postal Sales: Yes
Nearest Police Station: Fleming Way, Swindon
Police Telephone Nº: (01793) 528111

GROUND INFORMATION

Away Supporters' Entrances & Sections:
Castrol Stand turnstiles for the Castrol Stand

ADMISSION INFO (1996/97 PRICES)

Adult Seating: £10.00 – £13.50
Child Seating: £5.00 – £7.50
Programme Price: £1.50

DISABLED INFORMATION

Wheelchairs: 40 spaces in total for Home and Away fans in the disabled section, Rover Family Stand
Helpers: One helper admitted per disabled person
Prices: Free of charge for disabled. Helpers £5.00
Disabled Toilets: Available within the disabled area
Commentaries are available for the blind
Are Bookings Necessary: Yes
Contact: (01793) 430430

Travelling Supporters' Information:
Routes: From London, East and South: Exit M4 at Junction 15 and take A345 into Swindon along Queen's Drive. Take the 3rd exit at 'Magic Roundabout' into County Road; From West: Exit M4 at Junction 15 then as above; From North: Tale M4 or A345/A420/A361 to County Road roundabout, then as above.

TORQUAY UNITED FC

Founded: 1898 (**Entered League:** 1927)	**Colours:** Shirts – Yellow and Navy Stripes
Former Names: Torquay Town (1898-1910)	Shorts – Navy
Nickname: 'Gulls'	**Telephone Nº:** (01803) 328666
Ground: Plainmoor Ground, Torquay,	**Ticket Office:** (01803) 328666
TQ1 3PS	**Fax Number:** (01803) 232976
Record Attendance: 21,908 (29/1/55)	**Ground Capacity:** 5,987
Pitch Size: 110 × 74 yards	**Seating Capacity:** 2,324

ELLACOMBE END

HOMELANDS LANE / GRAND STAND

MARNHAM ROAD / POPULAR SIDE

(Away)
BABBACOMBE END
WARBRO ROAD

GENERAL INFORMATION

Supporters Club: c/o Mr T. Webb, 50 Carlton Road, Torquay
Telephone Nº: (01803) 297778
Car Parking: Street Parking
Coach Parking: Lymington Road Coach Station (½ mile)
Nearest Railway Station: Torquay (2 miles)
Nearest Bus Station: Lymington Road (½ mile)
Club Shop: At Ground
Opening Times: Matchdays & during Office Hours
Telephone Nº: (01803) 328666
Postal Sales: Yes
Nearest Police Station: Torquay (1 mile)
Police Telephone Nº: (0990) 777444

GROUND INFORMATION

Away Supporters' Entrances & Sections:
Babbacombe End turnstiles for Babbacombe End

ADMISSION INFO (1996/97 PRICES)

Adult Standing: £8.00
Adult Seating: £8.00
Child Standing: £4.00
Child Seating: £4.00
Programme Price: £1.30

DISABLED INFORMATION

Wheelchairs: 30 spaces in total in the disabled section, in front of Ellacombe End Stand
Helpers: One helper admitted per disabled person
Prices: Free of charge for Disabled and Helpers
Disabled Toilets: 2 available within the Main Stand
Audio facilities available for the blind
Are Bookings Necessary: No
Contact: (01803) 328666

Travelling Supporters' Information:
Routes: From North and East: Take M5 to A38 and A380 to Torquay. On entering Torquay, turn left at the 3rd set of traffic lights into Hele Road. Continue straight on over two mini-roundabouts and up West Hill Road to traffic lights, then go straight ahead into Warbro Road. The ground is situated 200 yards on the right.

TOTTENHAM HOTSPUR FC

Founded: 1882 **(Entered League:** 1908)
Former Names: Hotspur FC (1882-1885)
Nickname: 'Spurs'
Ground: White Hart Lane, 748 High
Road, Tottenham, London N17 0AP
Record Attendance: 75,038 (5/3/38)
Pitch Size: 110 × 73 yards

Colours: Shirts – White
Shorts – Navy Blue
Telephone N°: (0181) 365-5000
Ticket Office: (0181) 365-5050
Fax Number: (0181) 365-5005
Ground Capacity: 33,147 (All seats)

PARK LANE
SOUTH STAND (Away)

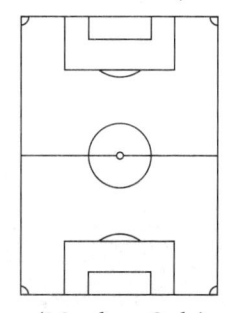

(Members Only)
NORTH STAND
PAXTON ROAD

GENERAL INFORMATION

Supporters Club: c/o Linda Watkins, Spurs
Members Club, 752B High Road, Tottenham N17
Telephone N°: (0181) 365-5150
Car Parking: None within ¼ mile
Coach Parking: Northumberland Park Coach Park,
Leeside Road
Nearest Railway Station: White Hart Lane
(Nearby)/Northumberland Park
Nearest Tube Station: Seven Sisters (Victoria);
Manor House (Piccadilly)
Club Shop: At Ground
Opening Times: Weekdays 9.30am – 5.30pm and
Matchdays 9.30am – 6.00pm
Telephone N°: (0181) 880-9019
Postal Sales: Yes
Nearest Police Station: Tottenham (1 mile)
Police Telephone N°: (0181) 801-3443

GROUND INFORMATION

Away Supporters' Entrances & Sections:
Park Lane entrances for South Stand

ADMISSION INFO (1996/97 PRICES)

Adult Seating: £17.00 – £33.00 (Members £15–£21)
Child Seating: £7.50 – £11.50 (Members only)
Programme Price: £1.80

DISABLED INFORMATION

Wheelchairs: 27 spaces for home fans, 17 for away
fans in the disabled areas. Home support: North
Stand Lower Tier; Away Support: South Stand
Helpers: One helper admitted per disabled person
Prices: Price for one disabled person + a helper –
£15.00 or £18.00
Disabled Toilets: 2 available in Paxton Road
Enclosure, 1 near Park Lane
Are Bookings Necessary: Yes
Contact: (0181) 365-5100

Travelling Supporters' Information:
Routes: From All Parts: Take A406 North Circular to Edmonton and at traffic lights follow signs for Tottenham
(A1010) into Fore Street for the ground.

TRANMERE ROVERS FC

Founded: 1881 (Entered League: 1921)
Former Names: Belmont FC
Nickname: 'Rovers'
Ground: Prenton Park, Prenton Road West, Birkenhead   L42 9PN
Record Attendance: 24,424 (5/2/72)
Pitch Size: 110 × 70 yards

Colours: Shirts – White
        Shorts – White
Telephone Nº: (0151) 608-3677/608-4194
Ticket Office: (0151) 609-0137
Fax Number: (0151) 608-4385
Ground Capacity: 16,800 (All seats)

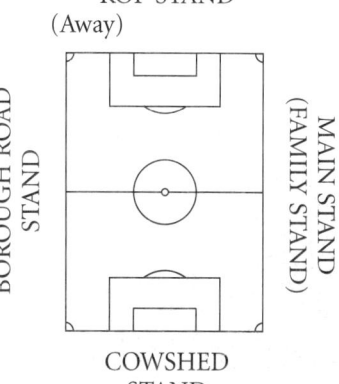

KOP STAND
(Away)

BOROUGH ROAD STAND

MAIN STAND (FAMILY STAND)

COWSHED STAND

GENERAL INFORMATION

Supporters Club: C. Dalziel, c/o The Club
Telephone Nº: (0151) 608-3677/608-4194
Car Parking: Large car park at ground (£3.00)
Coach Parking: At the ground (£10.00 charge)
Nearest Railway Station: Hamilton Square, Rock Ferry (1 mile)
Nearest Bus Station: Birkenhead
Club Shop: At Ground
Opening Times: Weekdays and Matchdays 9.00am – 5.00pm
Telephone Nº: (0151) 608-3677/608-4194
Postal Sales: Yes
Nearest Police Stat'n: Bebington (2 miles)
Police Telephone Nº: (0151) 709-6010

GROUND INFORMATION

Away Supporters' Entrances & Sections:
Kop Stand turnstiles 22-27 – access from Car Park

ADMISSION INFO (1996/97 PRICES)

Adult Seating: £10.00 – £11.50
Child Seating: £5.00 – £7.00
Programme Price: £1.50
Note: Concessionary admission available by prepaid vouchers

DISABLED INFORMATION

Wheelchairs: 28 spaces in total for Home and Away fans in the disabled section, Paddock – Family Stand
Helpers: One helper admitted per disabled person
Prices: Free of charge for disabled. Helpers £10.00
Disabled Toilets: 2 available in the disabled section
Are Bookings Necessary: Yes
Contact: (0151) 609-0137

Travelling Supporters' Information:
Routes: From North: Take Mersey Tunnel to M53, exit Junction 3 and take the 1st exit at the rounabout (A552), after 1¼ miles turn right at crossroads (B5151) then left into Prenton Road West; From South and East: Exit M53 at Junction 4 and take 4th exit at roundabout (B5151). After 2½ miles turn right into Prenton Road West.

WALSALL FC

Founded: 1888 **(Entered League:** 1892)
Former Names: Walsall Town Swifts FC
(1888-1895)
Nickname: 'Saddlers'
Ground: Bescot Stadium, Bescot Crescent
Walsall, West Midlands   WS1 4SA
Record Attendance: 10,628 (2/5/91)

Colours: Shirts – Red and White Stripes
   Shorts – Black
Telephone Nº: (01922) 22791
Ticket Office: (01922) 22791
Fax Number: (01922) 613202
Pitch Size: 110 × 73 yards
Ground Capacity: 9,000
Seating Capacity: 6,685

(BESCOT CRESCENT)
WILLIAM SHARP STAND

HIGHGATE STAND (Away)

H.L. FELLOWS STAND

GILBERT ALSO STAND

GENERAL INFORMATION

Supporters Club: c/o John Wilson, Saddlers Club,
Wallows Lane, Walsall
Telephone Nº: (01922) 22257
Car Parking: Car park at the ground
Coach Parking: At the ground
Nearest Railway Station: Bescot (adjacent)
Nearest Bus Station: Bradford Place, Walsall
Club Shop: At Ground
Opening Times: Weekdays and Matchdays 9.00am
– 5.30pm
Telephone Nº: (01922) 31072 (Town Centre)
Postal Sales: Yes
Nearest Police Station: Walsall (2 miles)
Police Telephone Nº: (01922) 38111

GROUND INFORMATION

Away Supporters' Entrances & Sections:
Highgate Stand turnstiles 1-4 for Highgate Stand

ADMISSION INFO (1996/97 PRICES)

Adult Standing: £8.00
Adult Seating: £10.00 – £12.00
Child Standing: £6.00
Child Seating: £8.00 – £12.00
Programme Price: £1.50

DISABLED INFORMATION

Wheelchairs: 30 spaces in total for Home and Away
fans in the disabled section, Highgate Stand
Helpers: One helper admitted per disabled person
Prices: Free of charge for disabled and helpers
Disabled Toilets: Adjacent to disabled viewing bays
Commentaries are available for the blind
Are Bookings Necessary: Yes
Contact: (01922) 22791

Travelling Supporters' Information:
Routes: From All Parts: Exit M6 at Junction 9 turning North towards Walsall onto the A461. After ¼ mile turn
right into Wallows Lane and pass over the railway bridge. Then tale 1st right into Bescot Crescent and the ground
is ½ mile along on the left adjacent to Bescot Railway Station.

WATFORD FC

Founded: 1891 (**Entered League:** 1920)
Former Names: Formed by amalgamation of West Herts FC and St. Mary's FC
Nickname: 'Hornets'
Ground: Vicarage Road Stadium, Watford WD1 8ER
Record Attendance: 34,099 (3/2/69)

Colours: Shirts – Yellow with black & red Shorts – Black
Telephone Nº: (01923) 496000
Ticket Office: (01923) 496010
Fax Number: (01923) 496001
Pitch Size: 115 × 75 yards
Ground Capacity: 22,000 (All seats)

VICARAGE ROAD
NORTH STAND

ROUS STAND (Away)

OCCUPATION ROAD
EAST STAND

SOUTH STAND

GENERAL INFORMATION

Supporters Club: c/o Marketing Department, c/o The Club
Telephone Nº: (01923) 496006
Car Parking: Nearby multi-storey car park
Coach Parking: Cardiff Road car park
Nearest Railway Station: Station at ground (Big Games only) or Watford Junction
Nearest Bus Station: Watford
Club Shop: At Ground
Opening Times: Monday to Saturday 9.00 – 5.00
Telephone Nº: (01923) 496005
Postal Sales: Yes
Nearest Police Station: Shady Lane, Clarendon Road, Watford (1½ miles)
Police Telephone Nº: (01923) 472000

GROUND INFORMATION

Away Supporters' Entrances & Sections:
South West corner entrances for Rous Stand Lower

ADMISSION INFO (1996/97 PRICES)

Adult Seating: £11.00 or £13.00
Child Seating: £8.00 or £13.00
Programme Price: £1.50

DISABLED INFORMATION

Wheelchairs: 40 spaces in total in the disabled sections, South East Corner and North Stand
Helpers: One helper admitted per disabled person
Prices: £6.00 for the disabled. £11.00 for helpers
Disabled Toilets: Adjacent to disabled enclosures
Commentaries available in East Stand – no charge
Are Bookings Necessary: No
Contact: (01923) 496010

Travelling Supporters' Information:
Routes: From North: Exit M1 Junction 5, take 2nd exit at roundabout (A41) signposted Harrow. Take 3rd exit at next roundabout to Hartspring Lane. Through traffic lights, continue straight ahead (now Aldenham Road) to next roundabout. Take 2nd exit (Aldenham Road), to next traffic lights. Go through lights, move into right-hand lane (marked Watford), follow one-way to Bushey Station, then moving to left-hand lane. Turn left under Bushey Arches into Eastbury Road. Turn right at traffic lights into Deacon Hill, continue to next traffic lights, turn left into Cardiff Road for stadium/coach park; From South: Exit M1 Junction 5, take 1st exit at roundabout (A41) then as North; From East: Exit M25 Junction 21A, join M1 Junction 6. Exit Junction 5 (then as North); From West: Exit M25 Junction 19, take 3rd exit at roundabout, A411 (Hempstead Road), signs Watford. After 2 miles go straight on at roundabout then 3rd exit (Rickmansworth Road) at next roundabout. Take 2nd turning left into Cassio Road. Through traffic lights to Merton Road, Wiggenhall Road. At traffic lights, right into Cardiff Road (then as North).

WEST BROMWICH ALBION FC

Founded: 1879 (**Entered League:** 1888)
Former Names: West Bromwich Strollers
(1879-1880)
Nickname: 'Throstles' 'Baggies' 'Albion'
Ground: The Hawthorns, Halfords Lane,
West Bromwich, West Midlands   B71 4LF
Record Attendance: 64,815 (6/3/37)

Colours: Shirts – Navy blue/white stripes
Shorts – White
Telephone Nº: (0121) 525-8888
Ticket Office: (0121) 553-5472
Fax Number: (0121) 553-6634
Pitch Size: 115 × 74 yards
Ground Capacity: 25,200 (All seats)

SMETHWICK END
(Away)

WEST BROMWICH BUILDING
SOCIETY FAMILY STAND

HALFORDS LANE
MAIN STAND

BIRMINGHAM
ROAD END

GENERAL INFORMATION
Supporters Club: c/o Alan Cleverley, 1 St.
Christophers, Hamstead Hill, Handsworth Wood,
Birmingham   B20 1BP
Telephone Nº: (0121) 551-6439
Car Parking: Halfords Lane Car Parks, W.B.B.S.
Stand Car Park
Coach Parking: W.B.B.S. Stand Car Park
Nearest Railway Station: Rolfe Street, Smethwick
(1½ miles), Hawthorns (200 yards)
Nearest Bus Station: Town Centre
Club Shop: At Ground
Opening Times: Weekdays 9.00am – 5.00pm and
Saturday Matchdays 9.00am – 2.45pm
Telephone Nº: (0121) 525-2145
Postal Sales: Yes
Nearest Police Station: Holyhead Road,
Handsworth (½ mile)
Police Telephone Nº: (0121) 554-3414

GROUND INFORMATION
Away Supporters' Entrances & Sections:
Smethwick End 'A' turnstiles
ADMISSION INFO (1996/97 PRICES)
Adult Seating: £11.00 – £16.00
Child Seating: £6.00 – £10.00
Programme Price: £1.50
DISABLED INFORMATION
Wheelchairs: 113 spaces in total in the disabled
sections, Birmingham Road End & Smethwick End
Helpers: One helper admitted per disabled person
Prices: Free of charge for disabled. Helpers £11.00
Disabled Toilets: Available within disabled section
Commentaries available for 6 people
Are Bookings Necessary: Yes
Contact: (0121) 525-8888

Travelling Supporters' Information:
Routes: From All Parts: Exit M5 at Junction 1 and follow Matchday signs for the ground. New traffic plan has
made the "obvious" route via A41 unusable on matchdays.

WEST HAM UNITED FC

Founded: 1895 (**Entered League:** 1919)	**Colours:** Shirts – Claret and Blue
Former Names: Thames Iron Works FC	Shorts – White
Nickname: 'Hammers'	**Telephone Nº:** (0181) 548-2748
Ground: Boleyn Ground, Green Street,	**Ticket Office:** (0181) 548-2700
Upton Park, London E13 9AZ	**Fax Number:** (0181) 471-2997
Record Attendance: 42,322 (17/10/70)	**Pitch Size:** 112 × 72 yards
	Ground Capacity: 26,014 (All seats)

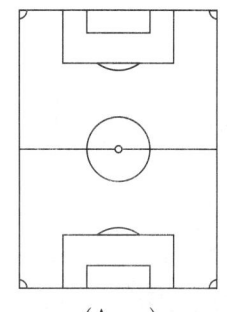

CASTLE STREET
BOBBY MOORE STAND

PRIORY ROAD EAST STAND

GREEN STREET WEST STAND

(Away)
CENTENARY STAND

GENERAL INFORMATION

Supporters Club: c/o Mr C. Rogers, West Ham Supporters' Club, Castle Street, East Ham, London E6 1PP
Telephone Nº: (0181) 472-1680
Car Parking: Street Parking
Coach Parking: By Police direction
Nearest Railway Station: Barking
Nearest Tube Station: Upton Park (5 minutes walk)
Club Shop: The Hammers Shop
Opening Times: Weekdays and Matchdays 9.30am – 5.00pm
Telephone Nº: (0181) 548-2748
Postal Sales: Yes
Nearest Police Station: East Ham High Street South (½ mile)
Police Telephone Nº: (0181) 593-8232

GROUND INFORMATION

Away Supporters' Entrances & Sections:
Turnstiles 1a – 6, Centenary Stand

ADMISSION INFO (1995/96 PRICES)

Adult Seating: £11.00 – £20.00
Child Seating: Concessions in Family Area
Programme Price: £1.50

DISABLED INFORMATION

Wheelchairs: 16 spaces for home fans, 4 spaces for away fans in the disabled area, West Stand
Helpers: Admitted
Prices: Free of charge for disabled. Helpers £5.00
Disabled Toilets: One available 50 yards from the disabled area
Are Bookings Necessary: Yes
Contact: (0181) 548-2748

Travelling Supporters' Information:
Routes: From North and West: Take North Circular (A406) to A124 (East Ham) then along Barking Road for approximately 1½ miles until approaching traffic lights at crossroad. Turn right into Green Street, the ground is on the right-hand side; From South: Take the Blackwall Tunnel and A13 to Canning Town. Follow signs for East Ham (A124). After 1¾ miles turn left into Green Street; From East: Take A13 and turn right onto A117 at crossroads. After approximately 1 mile turn left at crossroads onto A124. Turn right (¾ mile) into Green Street.

WIGAN ATHLETIC FC

Founded: 1932 (**Entered League**: 1978)
Former Names: None
Nickname: 'Latics'
Ground: Springfield Park, Wigan, Lancs.
WN6 7BA
Record Attendance: 27,500 (12/12/51)
Pitch Size: 117 × 73 yards

Colours: Shirts – Blue, White and Green
Shorts – Blue
Telephone Nº: (01942) 244433
Ticket Office: (01942) 244433
Fax Number: (01942) 494654
Ground Capacity: 6,901
Seating Capacity: 1,128

SHEVINGTON END
(Away)

PHOENIX STAND
(FAMILY STAND)

ST. ANDREWS DRIVE
POPULAR SIDE

TOWN END

GENERAL INFORMATION

Supporters Club: Joe Mills, c/o The Club
Telephone Nº: (01942) 243512
Car Parking: Street Parking
Coach Parking: Shevington End
Nearest Railway Station: Wallgate and North West
(1 mile)
Nearest Bus Station: Wigan
Club Shop: At Ground
Opening Times: Weekdays and Matchdays 9.00am
– 5.00pm
Telephone Nº: (01942) 244433
Postal Sales: Yes
Nearest Police Station: Harrogate Street (1 mile)
Police Telephone Nº: (01942) 244981

GROUND INFORMATION

Away Supporters' Entrances & Sections:
Shevington End (open)

ADMISSION INFO (1996/97 PRICES)

Adult Standing: £7.00
Adult Seating: £9.00
Child Standing: £4.00
Child Seating: £6.00 (£3.00 in the Family Stand)
Programme Price: £1.40

DISABLED INFORMATION

Wheelchairs: 10 spaces in total for Home and Away
fans in the disabled section, Family Enclosure
Helpers: One helper admitted per disabled person
Prices: Free of charge for Disabled and Helpers
Disabled Toilets: None
Commentaries are available in the Phoenix Stand
Are Bookings Necessary: Yes
Contact: (01942) 244433

Travelling Supporters' Information:
Routes: From North: Exit M6 at Junction 27 following signs for Wigan (A5209), turn right (¼ mile) (B5206).
Turn left after 1 mile and after 4½ miles take left turn into Springfield Road; From South: Exit M6 at Junction 25
following signs for Wigan (A49). Turn left into Robin Park Road and into Scot Lane. Turn right at the 3rd traffic
lights into Woodhouse Lane and left at the traffic lights into Springfield Road; From East: Take A557 into Town
Centre then left into Robin Park Road (then as South).

WIMBLEDON FC

Founded: 1889 (**Entered League:** 1977)	**Colours:** Shirts – Blue
Former Names: Wimbledon Old Centrals	Shorts – Blue
FC (1889-1905)	**Telephone Nº:** (0181) 771-2233
Nickname: 'Dons'	**Ticket Office:** (0181) 771-8841
Ground: Selhurst Park, London	**Fax Number:** (0181) 768-0640
SE25 6PY	**Pitch Size:** 110 × 74 yards
Record Attendance: 30,115 (1992-93)	**Ground Capacity:** 26,309 (All seats)

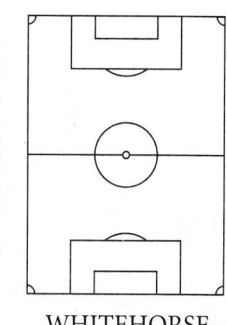

HOLMESDALE ROAD STAND

PARK ROAD (Away) / ARTHUR WAIT STAND

CLIFTON ROAD MAIN STAND

WHITEHORSE LANE STAND

GENERAL INFORMATION

Supporters Club: Sue Moody, c/o The Club
Telephone Nº: (0181) 771-2233
Car Parking: Street Parking
Coach Parking: Thornton Heath
Nearest Railway Station: Selhurst/Norwood Junction (5 minutes walk)
Nearest Bus Station: Norwood Junction
Club Shop: At Ground
Opening Times: Weekdays and Matchdays 9.30am –5.30pm
Telephone Nº: (0181) 653-5584
Postal Sales: Yes
Nearest Police Station: South Norwood (15 minutes walk)
Police Telephone Nº: (0181) 653-8568

GROUND INFORMATION

Away Supporters' Entrances & Sections:
Park Road turnstiles for Arthur Wait Stand

ADMISSION INFO (1996/97 PRICES)

Adult Seating: £8.00 – £20.00
Child Seating: £4.00 – £10.00
Prices vary according to category of match and ground position
Programme Price: £1.50

DISABLED INFORMATION

Wheelchairs: Unconfirmed number accommodated in the disabled area, Holmesdale Road Stand
Helpers: One helper admitted per disabled person
Prices: Free for the disabled. Concessionary prices for helpers
Disabled Toilets: Located in the disabled area
Commentaries are available for 12 people
Are Bookings Necessary: Yes
Contact: (0181) 771-8841

Travelling Supporters' Information:
Routes: From North: Take M1/A1 to North Circular (A406) to Chiswick. Then take the South Circular (A205) to Wandsworth and then the A3 to the A214 and follow signs to Streatham to the A23. Turn left onto the B273 after 1 mile, follow to the end and turn left into the High Street and into Whitehorse Lane; From East: Take A232 (Croydon Road) to Shirley and join A215 (Northwood Road). After 2¼ miles turn left into Whitehorse Lane; From South: Take A23 and follow signs for Crystal Palace (B266) through Thornton Heath into Whitehorse Lane; From West: Take the M4 to Chiswich (then as North).

WOLVERHAMPTON WANDERERS FC

Founded: 1877 **(Entered League:** 1888)
Former Names: St. Luke's FC & The
Wanderers FC (combined in 1880)
Nickname: 'Wolves'
Ground: Molineux Ground, Waterloo
Road, Wolverhampton WV1 4QR
Record Attendance: 61,315 (11/2/39)

Colours: Shirts – Gold
Shorts – Black
Telephone Nº: (01902) 655000
Ticket Office: (01902) 653653
Fax Number: (01902) 687003
Pitch Size: 116 × 74 yards
Ground Capacity: 28,500 (All seats)

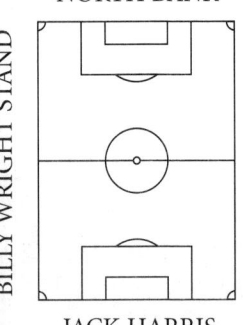

STAN CULLIS STAND
NORTH BANK

WATERLOO ROAD
BILLY WRIGHT STAND

JOHN IRELAND STAND
MOLINEUX STREET

JACK HARRIS
STAND

GENERAL INFORMATION

Supporters Club: Sue Glover, c/o Consumer Sales
Department, Molineux Ground, Waterloo Road,
Wolverhampton WV1 4QR
Telephone Nº: (01902) 656100
Car Parking: Around West Park and Rear of Stan
Cullis Stand
Coach Parking: By Police direction
Nearest Railway Station: Wolverhampton (1 mile)
Nearest Bus Station: Wolverhampton (¼ mile)
Club Shop: At Ground
Opening Times: Matchdays & Weekdays 9.00 – 5.00
Telephone Nº: (01902) 658777
Postal Sales: Yes
Nearest Police Station: Dunstall Road (500 yards)
Police Telephone Nº: (01902) 649000

GROUND INFORMATION

Away Supporters' Entrances & Sections:
Jack Harris turnstiles Block 5

ADMISSION INFO (1996/97 PRICES)

Adult Seating: £10.00 – £15.00
Child Seating: £6.50 – £9.50
Note: Members receive ticket discounts and other
concessions in the Family Area.
Programme Price: £1.50

DISABLED INFORMATION

Wheelchairs: 50 spaces in total for Home and Away
fans in the disabled section, Stan Cullis Stand
Helpers: One helper admitted per wheelchair
Prices: Free of charge for disabled. Helpers £6.00
Disabled Toilets: Toilets at both end of the Stan
Cullis Stand
Commentaries by a local blind organisation
Are Bookings Necessary: Yes
Contact: (01902) 658666

Travelling Supporters' Information:
Routes: From North: Exit M6 Junction 12, follow signs for Wolverhampton A5, then A449, take 2nd exit at
roundabout into Waterloo Road. Turn left into Molineux Street; From South: Exit M5 Junction 2, follow signs
for Wolverhampton A4123, turn right then left into Ring Road, turn left 1 mile into Waterloo Road, then right
into Molineux Street; From East: Exit M6 at Junction 10 following signs Wolverhampton A454, turn right at
crossroads into Stratford Street then left after ¼ mile into Ring Road, right at crossroads into Waterloo Road then
right into Molineux Street; From West: Take A454 and at roundabout turn left into Ring Road (then as East).

WREXHAM FC

Founded: 1873 (**Entered League:** 1921)	**Colours:** Shirts – Red
Former Names: None	Shorts – White
Nickname: 'Robins'	**Telephone N°:** (01978) 262129
Ground: Racecourse Ground, Mold	**Ticket Office:** (01978) 262129
Road, Wrexham, Clwyd LL11 2AH	**Fax Number:** (01978) 357821
Record Attendance: 34,445 (26/1/57)	**Ground Capacity:** 11,500
Pitch Size: 111 × 71 yards	**Seating Capacity:** 5,026

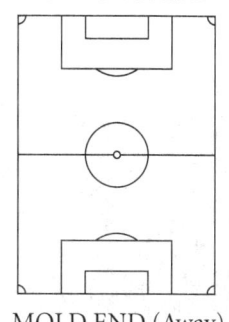

CRISPIN LANE
KOP TOWN END

(CAR PARK) YALE STAND

MOLD ROAD STAND (NOT IN USE)

MOLD END (Away)
MARSTONS STAND

GENERAL INFORMATION

Supporters Club: Miss Ena Williams, c/o The Club
Telephone N°: (01978) 262129
Car Parking: Town car parks nearby + Newi College (Mold End)
Coach Parking: –
Nearest Railway Station: Wrexham General (adjacent)
Nearest Bus Station: Wrexham (King Street)
Club Shop: Promotions Office, at the Ground
Opening Times: Office hours only
Telephone N°: (01978) 352536
Postal Sales: Yes
Nearest Police Station: Bodhyfryd (HQ) (1 mile)
Police Telephone N°: (01978) 290222

GROUND INFORMATION

Away Supporters' Entrances & Sections:
Mold End turnstiles for Marstons Stand (covered)

ADMISSION INFO (1996/97 PRICES)

Adult Standing: £8.00
Adult Seating: £11.00
Child Standing: £5.00
Child Seating: £8.00
Programme Price: £1.40

DISABLED INFORMATION

Wheelchairs: 18 spaces in total for Home and Away fans in the disabled section, Mold Road Side
Helpers: One helper admitted per wheelchair
Prices: Free of charge for disabled. Helpers £8.00
Disabled Toilets: Available in the disabled section
Are Bookings Necessary: Yes
Contact: (01978) 351332

Travelling Supporters' Information:
Routes: From North and West: Take A483 and Wrexham bypass to junction with A541. Branch left at the roundabout and follow Wrexham signs into Mold Road; From South and East: Take A525 or A534 into Wrexham then follow A541 signs into Mold Road.

WYCOMBE WANDERERS FC

Founded: 1884 (**Entered League:** 1993)
Former Names: None
Nickname: 'The Blues'; 'The Chairboys'
Ground: Adams Park, Hillbottom Road,
Sands, High Wycombe, Bucks
Record Attendance: 9,007 (7/1/95)
Pitch Size: 115 × 75 yards

Colours: Shirts – Dark/light blue quarters
Shorts – Navy blue
Telephone Nº: (01494) 472100
Ticket Office: (01494) 472100
Fax Number: (01494) 527633
Ground Capacity: Approximately 10,000
Seating Capacity: 6,207

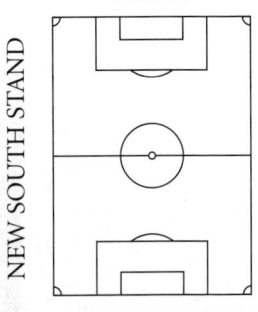

BUCKS FREE PRESS STAND

NEW SOUTH STAND

PITCHSIDE ENCLOSURE

MAIN STAND

HILLBOTTOM ROAD END
(AMERSHAM & WYCOMBE
COLLEGE END)

GENERAL INFORMATION
Supporters Club: None
Telephone Nº: –
Car Parking: Car park at the ground (320 cars)
Coach Parking: Car park at the ground
Nearest Railway Station: High Wycombe
Nearest Bus Station: High Wycombe
Club Shop: At the ground and also in Town
Opening Times: Weekdays and Matchdays
Telephone Nº: (01494) 472100 (Ground Shop);
(01494) 450957 (Town Shop)
Postal Sales: Yes
Nearest Police Station: Queen Victoria Road, High
Wycombe (2½ miles)
Police Telephone Nº: (01494) 465888

GROUND INFORMATION
Away Supporters' Entrances & Sections:
Amersham and Wycombe College End

ADMISSION INFO (1996/97 PRICES)
Adult Standing: £7.00
Adult Seating: £8.00 – £12.00
Child Standing: £4.50
Child Seating: £5.00 (Family Stand)
Programme Price: £1.50

DISABLED INFORMATION
Wheelchairs: 50 spaces in total available in the
disabled section of the Family Stand
Helpers: One helper admitted per wheelchair
Prices: £5.00 for the disabled. Full price for helpers
Disabled Toilets: Available in the New Family Stand
Commentaries are available for 5 people
Are Bookings Necessary: Yes
Contact: (01494) 472100

Travelling Supporters' Information:
Routes: From All Parts: Exit M40 at Junction 4 and take A4010 following Aylesbury signs. Go straight on at 3
mini-roundabouts and bear sharp left at 4th roundabout into Lane End Road. Fork right into Hillbottom Road
at the next roundabout. The ground is at the end of the road. Hillbottom Road is on the Sands Industrial
Estate; From Town Centre: Take A40 West and after 1½ miles turn left into Chapel Lane (after the traffic lights).
Turn right then right again at the mini-roundabout into Lane End Road – then as above.

YORK CITY FC

Founded: 1922 (**Entered League:** 1929)	**Colours:** Shirts – Red
Former Names: None	Shorts – Blue
Nickname: 'Minstermen'	**Telephone Nº:** (01904) 624447
Ground: Bootham Crescent, York	**Ticket Office:** (01904) 624447
YO3 7AQ	**Fax Number:** (01904) 631457
Record Attendance: 28,123 (5/3/38)	**Ground Capacity:** 9,534
Pitch Size: 115 × 74 yards	**Seating Capacity:** 3,509

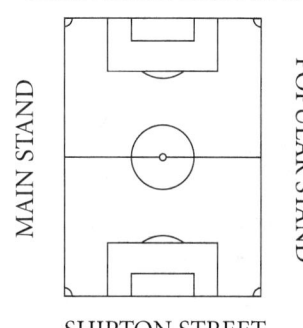

BOOTHAM CRESCENT (Away)
GROSVENOR ROAD END

MAIN STAND / POPULAR STAND

SHIPTON STREET

GENERAL INFORMATION

Supporters Club: c/o Raymond Wynn, 155 Manor Drive North, York
Telephone Nº: (01904) 797578
Car Parking: Street Parking
Coach Parking: By Police direction
Nearest Railway Station: York (1 mile)
Nearest Bus Station: York
Club Shop: At Ground
Opening Times: Monday to Wednesday 9.00am – 5.00pm; Thursday 9.00am – 5.00pm; Friday 9.00am – 4.30pm; Saturday Matches 1.00–3.00 & 4.40–5.30
Telephone Nº: (01904) 645941
Postal Sales: Yes
Nearest Police Station: Fulford
Police Telephone Nº: (01904) 631321

GROUND INFORMATION

Away Supporters' Entrances & Sections:
Grosvenor Road turnstiles for Grosvenor Road End

ADMISSION INFO (1996/97 PRICES)

Adult Standing: £7.50
Adult Seating: £7.50 – £10.00
Child Standing: £4.00 (Members only)
Child Seating: £4.00 – £6.00 (Members only)
Programme Price: £1.30

DISABLED INFORMATION

Wheelchairs: 18 spaces in total for Home and Away fans in the disabled section, in front of Family Stand
Helpers: One helper admitted per disabled person
Prices: Free of charge for disabled. Helpers £7.50
Disabled Toilets: Available at entrance to the disabled area
Commentaries are available for the blind
Are Bookings Necessary: No
Contact: (01904) 624447

Travelling Supporters' Information:
Routes: From North: Take A1 then A59 following York signs. Cross railway bridge and turn left after 2 miles into Water End. Turn right at the end following City Centre signs for nearly ½ mile then turn left into Bootham Crescent; From South: Take A64 and turn left after Buckles Inn onto Outer Ring Road. Turn right onto A19, follow City Centre signs for 1½ miles then turn left into Bootham Crescent; From East: Take Outer Ring Road turning left onto A19. Then as South; From West: Take Outer Ring Road turning right onto A19. Then as South.

THE F.A. CARLING PREMIERSHIP

and

THE ENDSLEIGH INSURANCE FOOTBALL LEAGUE

STATISTICS

1995-96

F.A. Carling Premiership Season 1995/96	Arsenal	Aston Villa	Blackburn Rvrs.	Bolton Wands	Chelsea	Coventry City	Everton	Leeds United	Liverpool	Manchester City	Manchester Utd.	Middlesbrough	Newcastle Utd.	Nott'm Forest	Q.P.R.	Sheffield Wed.	Southampton	Tottenham H.	West Ham Utd.	Wimbledon
Arsenal		2-0	0-0	2-1	1-1	1-1	1-2	2-1	0-0	3-1	1-0	1-1	2-0	1-1	3-0	4-2	4-2	0-0	1-0	1-3
Aston Villa	1-1		2-0	1-0	0-1	4-1	1-0	3-0	0-2	0-1	3-1	0-0	1-1	1-1	4-2	3-2	3-0	2-1	1-1	2-0
Blackburn Rvrs.	1-1	1-1		3-1	3-0	5-1	0-3	1-0	2-3	2-0	1-2	1-0	2-1	7-0	1-0	3-0	2-1	2-1	4-2	3-2
Bolton Wands.	1-0	0-2	2-1		2-1	1-2	1-1	0-2	0-1	1-1	0-6	1-1	1-3	1-1	0-1	2-1	0-1	2-3	0-3	1-0
Chelsea	1-0	1-2	2-3	3-2		2-2	0-0	4-1	2-2	1-1	1-4	5-0	1-0	1-0	1-1	0-0	3-0	0-0	1-2	1-2
Coventry City	0-0	0-3	5-0	0-2	1-0		2-1	0-0	1-0	2-1	0-4	0-0	0-1	1-1	1-0	0-1	1-1	2-3	2-2	3-3
Everton	0-2	1-0	1-0	3-0	1-1	2-2		2-0	1-1	2-0	2-3	4-0	1-3	3-0	2-0	2-2	2-0	1-1	3-0	2-4
Leeds United	0-3	2-0	0-0	0-1	1-0	3-1	2-2		1-0	0-1	3-1	0-1	0-1	1-3	1-3	2-0	1-0	1-3	2-0	1-1
Liverpool	3-1	3-0	3-0	5-2	2-0	0-0	1-2	5-0		6-0	2-0	1-0	4-3	4-2	1-0	1-0	1-1	0-0	2-0	2-2
Manchester City	0-1	1-0	1-1	1-0	0-1	1-1	0-2	0-0	2-2		2-3	0-1	3-3	1-1	2-0	1-0	2-1	1-1	2-1	1-0
Manchester Utd.	1-0	0-0	1-0	3-0	1-1	1-0	2-0	1-0	2-2	1-0		2-0	2-0	5-0	2-1	2-2	4-1	1-0	2-1	3-1
Middlesborough	2-3	0-2	2-0	1-4	2-0	2-1	0-2	1-1	2-1	4-1	0-3		1-2	1-1	1-0	3-1	0-0	0-1	4-2	1-2
Newcastle Utd.	2-0	1-0	1-0	2-1	2-0	3-0	1-0	2-1	2-1	3-1	0-1	1-0		3-1	2-1	2-0	1-0	1-1	3-0	6-1
Nott'm Forest	0-1	1-1	1-5	3-2	0-0	0-0	3-2	2-1	1-0	3-0	1-1	1-0	1-1		3-0	1-0	1-0	2-1	1-1	4-1
Q.P.R.	1-1	1-0	0-1	2-1	1-2	1-1	3-1	1-2	1-2	1-0	1-1	1-1	2-3	1-1		0-3	3-0	2-3	3-0	0-3
Sheffield Wed.	1-0	2-0	2-1	4-2	0-0	4-3	2-5	6-2	1-1	1-1	0-0	0-1	0-2	1-3	1-3		2-2	1-3	0-1	2-1
Southampton	0-0	0-1	1-0	1-0	2-3	1-0	2-2	1-1	1-3	1-1	3-1	2-1	1-0	3-4	2-0	0-1		0-0	0-0	0-0
Tottenham Hotsp.	2-1	0-1	2-3	2-2	1-1	3-1	0-0	2-1	1-3	1-0	4-1	1-1	1-1	0-1	1-0	1-0	1-0		0-1	3-1
West Ham Utd.	0-1	1-4	1-1	1-0	1-3	3-2	2-1	1-2	0-0	4-2	0-1	2-0	2-0	1-0	1-0	1-1	2-1	1-1		1-1
Wimbledon	0-3	3-3	1-1	3-2	1-1	0-2	2-3	2-4	1-0	3-0	2-4	0-0	3-3	1-0	2-1	2-2	1-2	0-1	0-1	

Manchester Utd.	38	25	7	6	73	35	82
Newcastle Utd.	38	24	6	8	66	37	78
Liverpool	38	20	11	7	70	34	71
Aston Villa	38	18	9	11	52	35	63
Arsenal	38	17	12	9	49	32	63
Everton	38	17	10	11	64	44	61
Blackburn Rvrs.	38	18	7	13	61	47	61
Tottenham H.	38	16	13	9	50	38	61
Nottingham For.	38	15	13	10	50	54	58
West Ham United	38	14	9	15	43	52	51
Chelsea	38	12	14	12	46	44	50
Middlesborough	38	11	10	17	35	50	43
Leeds United	38	12	7	19	40	57	43
Wimbledon	38	10	11	17	55	70	41
Sheffield Wed.	38	10	10	18	48	61	40
Coventry City	38	8	14	16	42	60	38
Southampton	38	9	11	18	34	52	38
Manchester City	38	9	11	18	33	58	38
Q.P.R.	38	9	6	23	38	57	33
Bolton Wands.	38	8	5	25	39	71	29

Champions : - Manchester United

Relegated : - Manchester City, Queen's Park Rangers and Bolton Wanderers

Endsleigh First Division Season 1995/96	Barnsley	Birmingham C.	Charlton Ath.	Crystal Palace	Derby County	Grimsby Town	Huddersfield T.	Ipswich Town	Leicester City	Luton Town	Millwall	Norwich City	Oldham Athletic	Port Vale	Portsmouth	Reading	Sheffield Utd.	Southend Utd.	Stoke City	Sunderland	Tranmere R.	Watford	West Brom A.	Wolverhampton
Barnsley		0-5	1-2	1-1	2-0	1-1	3-0	3-3	2-2	1-0	3-1	2-2	2-1	1-1	0-0	0-1	2-2	1-1	3-1	0-1	2-1	2-1	1-1	1-0
Birmingham City	0-0		3-4	0-0	1-4	3-1	2-0	3-1	2-2	4-0	2-2	3-1	0-0	3-1	2-0	1-2	0-1	2-0	1-1	0-2	1-0	1-0	1-1	2-0
Charlton Athletic	1-1	3-1		0-0	0-0	0-1	2-1	0-2	0-1	1-1	2-0	1-1	1-1	2-2	2-1	2-1	1-1	0-3	2-1	1-1	0-0	2-1	4-1	1-1
Crystal Palace	4-3	3-2	1-1		0-0	5-0	0-0	1-1	0-1	2-0	1-2	0-1	2-2	2-2	0-0	0-2	0-0	2-0	1-1	0-1	2-1	4-0	1-0	3-2
Derby County	4-1	1-1	2-0	2-1		1-1	3-2	1-1	0-1	1-1	2-2	2-1	2-1	0-0	3-2	3-0	4-2	1-0	3-1	3-1	6-2	1-1	3-0	0-0
Grimsby Town	3-1	2-1	1-2	0-2	1-1		1-1	3-1	2-2	0-0	1-2	2-2	1-1	1-0	2-1	0-0	0-2	1-1	1-0	0-4	1-1	0-0	1-0	3-0
Huddersfield T.	3-0	4-2	2-2	3-0	0-1	1-3		2-1	3-1	1-0	3-0	3-2	0-0	0-2	0-1	3-1	1-2	3-1	1-1	1-1	1-0	1-0	4-1	2-1
Ipswich Town	2-2	2-0	1-5	1-0	1-0	2-2	2-1		4-2	0-1	0-0	2-1	2-1	5-1	3-2	1-2	1-1	1-1	4-1	3-0	1-2	4-2	2-1	1-2
Leicester City	2-2	3-0	1-1	2-3	0-0	2-1	2-1	0-2		1-1	2-1	3-2	2-0	1-1	4-2	1-1	0-2	1-3	2-3	0-0	0-1	1-0	1-2	1-0
Luton Town	1-3	0-0	0-1	0-0	1-2	3-2	2-2	1-2	1-1		1-0	1-3	1-1	3-2	3-1	1-2	1-0	3-1	1-2	0-2	3-2	0-0	1-2	2-3
Millwall	0-1	2-0	0-2	1-4	0-1	2-1	0-0	2-1	1-1	1-0		2-1	0-1	1-2	1-1	1-1	1-0	0-0	2-3	1-2	2-2	1-2	2-1	0-1
Norwich City	3-1	1-1	0-1	1-0	1-0	2-2	2-0	2-1	0-1	0-1	0-0		2-1	2-1	1-1	3-3	0-0	0-1	0-0	1-1	1-2	2-2	2-2	2-3
Oldham Athletic	0-1	4-0	1-1	3-1	0-1	1-0	3-0	1-1	3-1	1-0	2-2	2-0		2-2	1-1	2-1	2-1	0-1	2-0	1-2	1-2	0-0	1-2	0-0
Port Vale	3-0	1-2	1-3	1-2	1-1	1-0	1-0	2-1	0-2	1-0	0-1	1-0	1-3		0-2	3-2	2-3	2-1	1-0	1-1	1-1	1-1	3-1	2-1
Portsmouth	0-0	0-1	2-1	2-3	2-2	3-1	1-1	0-1	2-1	4-0	0-1	1-0	2-1	1-2		0-0	1-2	4-2	3-3	2-2	0-2	4-2	0-2	0-2
Reading	0-0	0-1	0-0	0-2	3-2	0-2	3-1	1-4	3-1	1-0	3-1	0-3	2-0	2-2	0-1		0-3	3-3	1-0	1-0	0-0	3-1	0-0	3-0
Sheffield United	1-0	1-1	2-0	2-3	0-2	1-2	0-2	2-2	1-3	1-0	2-0	2-1	2-1	1-1	4-1	0-0		3-0	0-0	0-0	0-2	1-1	1-2	2-1
Southend United	0-0	3-1	1-1	1-1	1-2	1-0	0-0	2-1	2-1	0-1	2-0	1-1	1-1	2-1	2-1	0-0	2-1		2-4	0-2	2-0	1-1	2-1	2-1
Stoke City	2-0	1-0	1-2	1-1	1-1	1-2	1-1	3-1	1-0	5-0	1-1	0-1	1-1	0-1	2-1	1-1	2-2	1-0		1-0	0-0	2-0	2-1	1-0
Sunderland	2-1	3-0	0-0	1-0	3-0	1-0	3-2	1-0	1-2	1-0	6-0	0-1	1-0	0-0	1-1	2-2	2-0	1-0	0-0		0-0	1-1	0-0	2-0
Tranmere Rvrs.	1-3	2-2	0-0	2-3	5-1	0-1	3-1	5-2	1-1	1-0	2-2	1-1	2-0	2-1	1-2	2-1	1-1	3-0	0-0	2-0		2-3	2-2	2-2
Watford	2-3	1-1	1-2	0-0	0-0	6-3	0-1	2-3	0-1	1-1	0-1	0-2	2-1	5-2	1-2	4-2	2-1	2-2	3-0	3-3	3-0		1-1	1-1
West Brom Alb.	2-1	1-0	1-0	2-3	3-2	3-1	1-2	0-0	2-3	0-2	1-0	1-4	1-0	1-1	2-1	1-0	3-1	3-1	0-1	0-1	1-1	4-4		0-0
Wolverhampton	2-2	3-2	0-0	0-2	3-0	4-1	0-0	2-2	2-3	0-0	1-1	0-2	1-3	0-1	2-2	1-1	1-0	2-0	1-4	3-0	2-1	3-0	1-1	

Sunderland	46	22	17	7	59	33	83		Portsmouth	46	13	13	20	61	69	52
Derby County	46	21	16	8	69	48	79		Millwall	46	13	13	20	43	63	52
Crystal Palace	46	20	15	11	67	48	75		Watford	46	10	18	18	62	70	48
Stoke City	46	20	13	13	60	49	73		Luton Town	46	11	12	23	40	64	45
Leicester City	46	19	14	13	66	60	71
Charlton Athletic	46	17	20	9	57	45	71
Ipswich Town	46	19	12	15	79	69	69
Huddersfield T.	46	17	12	17	61	58	63
Sheffield United	46	16	14	16	57	54	62
Barnsley	46	14	18	14	60	66	60
West Brom. Alb.	46	16	12	18	60	68	60
Port Vale	46	15	15	16	59	66	60
Tranmere Rvrs.	46	14	17	15	64	60	59
Southend United	46	15	14	17	52	61	59
Birmingham City	46	15	13	18	61	64	58
Norwich City	46	14	15	17	59	55	57
Grimsby Town	46	14	14	18	55	69	56
Oldham Athletic	46	14	14	18	54	50	56
Reading	46	13	17	16	54	63	56
Wolverhampton	46	13	16	17	56	62	55

PROMOTION PLAY-OFFS

Charlton Athletic	1	Crystal Palace	2
Leicester City	0	Stoke City	0

Crystal Palace	1	Charlton Athletic	0

Crystal Palace win 3-1 on aggregate

Stoke City	0	Leicester City	1

Leicester City win 1-0 on aggregate

Crystal Palace	1	Leicester City	2

After extra-time. (Normal-time 1-1)

Promoted : - Sunderland, Derby County & Leicester City
Relegated : - Millwall, Watford & Luton Town

Endsleigh Second Division Season 1995/96

	Blackpool	Bournemouth	Bradford City	Brentford	Brighton & H.A.	Bristol City	Bristol Rovers	Burnley	Carlisle Utd.	Chesterfield	Crewe Alex.	Hull City	Notts County	Oxford United	Peterborough	Rotherham Utd.	Shrewsbury T.	Stockport Co.	Swansea City	Swindon Town	Walsall	Wrexham	Wycombe W.	York City
Blackpool	█	2-1	4-1	1-0	2-1	3-0	3-0	3-1	3-1	0-0	2-1	1-1	1-0	1-1	2-1	1-2	2-1	0-1	4-0	1-1	1-2	2-0	1-1	1-3
Bournemouth	1-0	█	3-1	1-0	3-1	1-1	2-1	0-2	2-0	2-0	0-4	2-0	0-2	0-1	3-0	2-1	0-2	3-2	3-1	0-0	0-0	1-1	2-3	2-2
Bradford City	2-1	1-0	█	2-1	1-3	3-0	2-3	2-2	3-1	2-1	2-1	1-1	1-0	1-0	2-1	2-0	3-1	0-1	5-1	1-1	1-0	2-0	0-4	2-2
Brentford	1-2	2-0	2-1	█	0-1	2-2	0-0	1-0	1-1	1-2	2-1	1-0	0-0	1-0	3-0	1-1	0-2	1-0	0-0	0-2	1-0	1-0	1-0	2-0
Brighton & H.A.	1-2	2-0	0-0	0-0	█	0-2	2-0	1-0	1-0	0-2	2-2	4-0	1-0	1-2	1-2	1-1	2-2	1-1	0-2	1-3	0-3	2-2	1-2	1-3
Bristol City	1-1	3-0	2-1	0-0	0-1	█	0-2	0-1	1-1	2-1	3-2	4-0	0-2	0-2	0-1	4-3	2-0	1-0	1-0	0-0	0-2	3-1	0-0	1-1
Bristol Rovers	1-1	0-2	1-0	2-0	1-0	2-4	█	1-0	1-1	1-0	1-2	2-1	0-3	2-0	1-1	1-0	2-1	1-3	2-2	1-4	2-0	1-2	2-1	1-0
Burnley	0-1	0-0	2-3	1-0	3-0	0-0	0-1	█	2-0	2-2	0-1	2-1	3-4	0-2	2-1	2-1	2-1	4-3	3-0	0-0	1-1	2-2	1-1	3-3
Carlisle United	1-2	4-0	2-2	2-1	1-0	2-1	1-2	2-0	█	1-1	1-0	2-0	0-0	1-2	1-1	2-0	1-1	0-1	3-0	0-1	1-1	1-2	4-2	2-0
Chesterfield	1-0	3-0	2-1	2-2	1-0	1-1	2-1	4-2	3-0	█	1-2	0-0	1-0	1-0	1-1	3-0	1-0	1-2	3-2	1-3	1-1	1-1	3-1	2-1
Crewe Alex.	1-2	2-0	1-2	3-1	3-1	4-2	1-2	3-1	3-0	1-0	█	1-0	2-2	1-2	2-0	2-1	3-0	0-1	4-1	0-2	1-0	0-0	2-0	1-1
Hull City	2-1	1-1	2-3	0-1	0-0	2-3	1-3	3-0	2-5	0-0	1-2	█	0-0	0-0	2-3	1-4	2-3	1-1	0-0	0-1	1-0	1-1	4-2	0-3
Notts County	1-1	2-0	0-2	4-0	2-1	2-2	4-2	1-1	3-1	4-1	0-1	1-0	█	1-1	1-0	2-1	1-1	1-0	4-0	1-3	2-1	1-0	2-0	2-2
Oxford United	1-0	2-0	2-0	2-1	1-1	2-0	1-2	5-0	4-0	1-0	1-0	2-0	1-1	█	4-0	1-1	6-0	2-1	5-1	3-0	3-2	0-0	1-4	2-0
Peterborough	0-0	4-5	3-1	0-1	3-1	1-1	0-0	0-2	6-1	0-1	3-1	3-1	0-1	1-1	█	1-0	2-2	0-1	1-1	0-2	2-3	1-0	3-0	6-1
Rotherham Utd.	2-1	1-0	2-0	1-0	1-0	2-3	1-0	1-0	2-2	0-1	2-2	1-2	2-0	1-0	5-1	█	2-2	2-0	1-1	0-2	0-1	0-1	0-0	2-2
Shrewsbury T.	0-2	1-2	1-1	2-1	2-1	4-1	1-1	3-0	1-1	0-0	2-3	1-1	0-1	2-0	1-1	3-1	█	1-2	1-2	1-2	0-2	2-2	1-1	2-1
Stockport Co.	1-1	3-1	1-2	1-1	3-1	3-0	0-0	2-0	0-1	1-1	0-0	4-2	0-1	1-1	0-2	2-0	1-0	█	2-0	1-1	0-1	2-3	1-1	3-0
Swansea City	0-2	1-1	2-0	2-1	2-1	2-1	2-2	2-4	1-1	3-2	2-1	0-0	0-0	1-1	0-0	0-0	3-1	0-3	█	0-1	2-1	1-3	1-2	0-1
Swindon Town	1-1	2-2	4-1	2-2	3-2	2-0	2-1	0-0	2-1	1-1	3-1	1-0	1-1	2-0	1-0	0-1	0-0	3-0	1-0	█	1-1	1-1	0-0	3-0
Walsall	1-1	0-0	2-1	0-1	2-1	2-1	1-1	3-1	2-1	3-0	3-2	0-0	2-2	1-1	3-1	3-0	0-2	4-1	0-0	1-1	█	1-2	0-1	1-0
Wrexham	1-1	5-0	1-2	2-2	1-1	0-0	3-2	0-2	3-2	3-0	2-3	5-0	1-1	2-1	1-0	7-0	1-1	2-3	1-0	4-3	3-0	█	1-0	2-3
Wycombe W.	0-1	1-2	5-2	2-1	0-2	1-1	1-1	4-1	4-0	1-0	1-1	2-2	1-1	0-3	1-1	1-1	2-0	4-1	0-1	1-2	1-0	1-1	█	2-1
York City	0-1	3-1	0-3	2-2	3-1	0-1	0-1	1-1	1-1	0-1	2-3	0-1	1-3	1-0	3-1	2-2	1-2	2-2	0-0	2-0	1-0	2-1	1-0	█

Swindon Town	46	25	17	4	71	34	92
Oxford United	46	24	11	11	76	39	83
Blackpool	46	23	13	10	67	40	82
Notts County	46	21	15	10	63	39	78
Crewe Alex.	46	22	7	17	77	60	73
Bradford City	46	22	7	17	71	69	73
Chesterfield	46	20	12	14	56	51	72
Wrexham	46	18	16	12	76	55	70
Stockport Co.	46	19	13	14	61	47	70
Bristol Rovers	46	20	10	16	57	60	70
Walsall	46	19	12	15	60	45	69
Wycombe W.	46	15	15	16	63	59	60
Bristol City	46	15	15	16	55	60	60
Bournemouth	46	16	10	20	51	70	58
Brentford	46	15	13	18	43	49	58
Rotherham Utd.	46	14	14	18	54	62	56
Burnley	46	14	13	19	56	68	55
Shrewsbury T.	46	13	14	19	58	70	53
Peterborough U.	46	13	13	20	59	66	52
York City	46	13	13	20	58	73	52
Carlisle United	46	12	13	21	57	72	49
Swansea City	46	11	14	21	43	79	47
Brighton & H.A.	46	10	10	26	46	69	40
Hull City	46	5	16	25	36	78	31

PROMOTION PLAY-OFFS

Bradford City 0	Blackpool 2
Crewe Alexandra 2	Notts County 2

Blackpool 0	Bradford City 3

Bradford City won 3-2 on aggregate

Notts County 1	Crewe Alexandra 0

Notts County won 3-2 on aggregate

Bradford City 2	Notts County 0

Promoted : - Swindon Town, Oxford United & Bradford City

Relegated : - Carlisle United, Swansea City, Brighton and Hove Albion & Hull City

Endsleigh Third Division Season 1995/96

	Barnet	Bury	Cambridge U.	Cardiff C.	Chester C.	Colchester U.	Darlington	Doncaster R.	Exeter City	Fulham	Gillingham	Hartlepool	Hereford U.	Leyton Orient	Lincoln City	Mansfield T.	Northampton T.	Plymouth Arg.	Preston N.E.	Rochdale	Scarborough	Scunthorpe U.	Torquay U.	Wigan Ath.
Barnet		0-0	2-0	1-0	1-1	1-1	1-1	1-1	3-2	3-0	0-2	5-1	1-3	3-0	3-1	0-0	2-0	1-2	1-0	0-4	1-0	1-0	4-0	5-0
Bury	0-0		1-2	3-0	1-1	0-0	0-0	4-1	2-0	3-0	1-0	0-3	2-0	2-1	7-1	0-2	0-1	0-5	0-0	1-1	0-2	3-0	1-0	2-1
Cambridge Utd.	1-1	2-4		4-2	1-1	3-1	0-1	2-2	1-1	0-0	0-0	0-1	2-2	2-0	2-1	0-2	0-1	2-3	2-1	2-1	4-1	1-2	1-1	2-1
Cardiff City	1-1	0-1	1-1		0-0	1-2	0-2	3-2	0-1	1-4	2-0	2-0	3-2	0-0	1-1	3-0	0-1	0-1	0-1	1-0	2-1	0-1	0-0	3-0
Chester City	0-2	1-1	1-1	4-0		1-1	4-1	0-3	2-2	1-1	1-1	2-0	2-1	1-1	5-1	2-1	1-0	3-1	1-1	1-2	5-0	3-0	4-1	0-0
Colchester Utd.	3-2	1-0	2-1	1-0	1-2		1-1	1-0	1-1	2-2	1-1	4-1	2-0	0-0	3-0	1-3	1-0	2-1	2-2	1-0	1-1	2-1	3-1	1-2
Darlington	1-1	4-0	0-0	0-1	3-1	2-2		1-2	1-0	1-1	1-0	1-0	1-0	2-0	3-2	1-1	1-2	2-0	1-2	0-1	1-2	0-0	1-2	2-1
Doncaster Rvrs.	1-0	0-1	2-1	0-0	1-2	3-2	1-2		2-0	0-2	0-1	1-0	0-0	4-1	1-1	0-0	1-0	0-0	2-2	0-3	1-0	2-0	1-0	2-1
Exeter City	1-0	1-1	1-0	2-0	1-2	2-2	0-1	1-0		2-1	0-0	1-0	0-2	2-2	1-1	2-2	1-1	1-1	2-0	2-0	1-0	0-0	0-4	
Fulham	1-1	0-0	0-2	4-2	2-0	1-1	2-2	3-1	2-1		0-0	2-2	0-0	2-1	1-2	4-2	1-3	4-0	2-2	1-1	1-0	1-3	4-0	1-0
Gillingham	1-0	3-0	3-0	1-0	3-1	0-1	0-0	4-0	1-0	1-0		2-0	1-1	1-1	2-0	2-0	0-0	1-0	1-1	1-0	1-0	0-0	2-0	2-1
Hartlepool Utd.	0-0	1-2	1-2	2-1	2-1	2-1	1-1	0-1	0-0	1-0	1-1		0-1	4-1	3-0	1-1	2-1	2-2	0-2	1-1	1-1	2-0	2-2	1-2
Hereford Utd.	4-1	3-4	5-2	1-3	1-0	1-1	0-1	1-0	2-2	1-0	0-0	4-1		3-2	1-0	0-1	1-0	3-0	0-1	2-0	0-0	3-0	2-1	2-2
Leyton Orient	3-3	0-2	3-1	4-1	0-2	0-1	1-1	3-1	0-3	1-0	0-1	4-1	0-1		2-0	1-0	2-0	0-1	0-2	2-0	1-0	0-0	1-0	1-1
Lincoln City	1-2	2-2	1-3	0-1	0-0	0-0	0-2	4-0	0-1	4-0	0-3	1-1	2-1	1-0		2-1	1-0	0-0	0-0	1-2	3-1	2-2	5-0	2-4
Mansfield Town	2-1	1-5	2-1	1-1	3-4	1-2	2-2	0-0	1-1	0-1	0-1	3-1	2-1	0-0	1-2		0-0	1-1	0-0	2-2	2-0	1-1	2-0	1-0
Northampton T.	0-2	4-1	3-0	1-0	1-0	2-1	1-1	3-3	0-0	2-0	1-1	0-0	1-1	1-2	1-1	3-3		1-0	1-2	2-1	2-0	1-2	1-1	0-0
Plymouth Argyle	1-1	1-0	1-0	0-0	4-2	1-1	0-1	3-1	2-2	3-0	1-0	3-0	0-1	1-1	3-0	1-0	1-0		0-2	2-0	5-1	1-3	4-3	3-1
Preston N.E.	0-1	0-0	3-3	5-0	2-0	2-0	1-1	1-0	2-0	1-1	0-0	3-0	2-2	4-0	1-2	6-0	0-3	3-2		1-2	3-2	2-2	1-0	1-1
Rochdale	0-4	1-1	3-1	3-3	1-3	1-1	1-2	1-0	4-2	1-1	2-0	4-0	0-0	1-0	3-3	1-1	1-2	0-1	0-3		0-2	1-1	3-0	0-2
Scarborough	1-1	0-2	2-0	1-0	0-0	0-0	1-2	0-2	0-0	2-2	0-2	1-2	2-2	2-1	0-0	1-1	2-1	2-2	1-2	1-1		1-4	2-1	0-0
Scunthorpe Utd.	2-0	1-2	1-2	1-1	0-2	1-0	3-3	2-2	4-0	3-1	1-1	2-1	0-1	2-0	2-3	1-1	0-0	1-1	1-2	1-3	3-3		1-0	3-1
Torquay United	1-1	0-2	0-3	0-0	1-1	2-3	0-1	1-2	0-2	2-1	0-0	0-1	1-2	3-0	0-2	0-4	1-0	0-0	1-8					1-1
Wigan Athletic	1-0	1-2	3-1	3-1	2-1	2-0	1-1	2-0	1-0	1-1	2-1	1-0	2-1	1-0	1-1	2-6	1-2	0-1	0-1	2-0	2-0	2-1	3-0	

Team	P	W	D	L	F	A	Pts
Preston N.E.	46	23	17	6	78	38	86
Gillingham	46	22	17	7	49	20	83
Bury	46	22	13	11	66	48	79
Plymouth Argyle	46	22	12	12	68	40	78
Darlington	46	20	18	8	60	42	78
Hereford United	46	20	14	12	65	47	74
Colchester Utd.	46	18	18	10	61	51	72
Chester City	46	18	16	12	72	53	70
Barnet	46	18	16	12	65	45	70
Wigan Athletic	46	20	10	16	62	56	70
Northampton T.	46	18	13	15	51	44	67
Scunthorpe Utd.	46	15	15	16	67	61	60
Doncaster Rvrs.	46	16	11	19	49	60	59
Exeter City	46	13	18	15	46	53	57
Rochdale	46	14	13	19	57	61	55
Cambridge Utd.	46	14	12	20	61	71	54
Fulham	46	12	17	17	57	63	53
Lincoln City	46	13	14	19	57	73	53
Mansfield Town	46	11	20	15	54	64	53
Hartlepool Utd.	46	12	13	21	47	67	49
Leyton Orient	46	12	11	23	44	63	47
Cardiff City	46	11	12	23	41	64	45
Scarborough	46	8	16	22	39	69	40
Torquay United	46	5	14	27	30	84	29

PROMOTION PLAY-OFFS

Colchester United 1   Plymouth Argyle 0
Hereford United 1   Darlington 2

Plymouth Argyle 3   Colchester United 1
Plymouth Argyle win 3-2 on aggregate
Darlington 2   Hereford United 1
Darlington win 4-2 on aggregate

Plymouth Argyle 1   Darlington 0

Promoted : - Preston North End, Gillingham, Bury and Plymouth Argyle

Relegated : - No relegation

A fresh insight into British football...

THE MONTHLY REVIEW OF BRITISH FOOTBALL

A MONTHLY MAGAZINE PROFILING CLUBS, GROUNDS & PLAYERS

THE PRESENT, THE PAST, THE FUTURE!

- Previews and Reviews
- Football Nostalgia
- Up-to-date Ground Development News
- Statistical Snap-shots
- Scottish & Non-League Sections
- And Much More!

What they have said about us : -

"A football fan's delight every month is WINGER" - *Programme Monthly*
"WINGER presents a lively coverage of our game" - *Association of Football Statisticians*
"WINGER is still an excellent publication" - *Football Programme Directory*

Subscription rates for 12 issues: **UK £18** *Overseas £25*

All Cheques payable to WINGER at :

Department S
WINGER
200 BRADFORD ROAD
OTLEY
LS21 3LT
ENGLAND

SEE IT FOR YOURSELF! If you wish to receive WINGER on a trial basis we will send you the current issue plus one extra past issue for £2.
Please send your cheque to the above address.

ENGLAND INTERNATIONAL LINE-UPS AND STATISTICS 1995

15 February 1995
v EIRE *Dublin*
Seaman	Arsenal
Barton	Wimbledon
Adams	Arsenal
Pallister	Manchester United
Le Saux	Blackburn Rovers
Ince	Manchester United
Anderton	Tottenham Hotspur
Platt	Sampdoria
Beardsley	Newcastle United
Le Tissier	Southampton
Shearer	Blackburn Rovers

Result 0-1 (Abandoned after 27 minutes – crowd trouble)

29 March 1995
v URUGUAY *Wembley*
Flowers	Blackburn Rovers
Jones	Liverpool
Adams	Arsenal
Pallister	Manchester United
Le Saux	Blackburn R. (sub McManaman)
Venison	Newcastle United
Platt	Sampdoria
Anderton	Tottenham
Barnes	Liverpool
Sheringham	Tottenham (sub Cole)
Beardsley	Newcastle United (sub Barmby)

Result 0-0

3 June 1995
v JAPAN *Wembley*
Flowers	Blackburn Rovers
Neville	Manchester United
Scales	Liverpool
Unsworth	Everton
Pearce	Nottingham Forest
Batty	Blackburn R. (sub Gascoigne)
Anderton	Tottenham
Platt	Sampdoria
Beardsley	Newcastle U. (sub McManaman)
Collymore	Nottm. For. (sub Sheringham)
Shearer	Blackburn Rovers

Result 2-1 Anderton, Platt (pen)

8 June 1995
v SWEDEN *Elland Road, Leeds*
Flowers	Blackburn Rovers
Barton	Wimbledon
Cooper	Nottingham Forest
Pallister	Manchester Utd. (sub Scales)
Le Saux	Blackburn Rovers
Anderton	Tottenham
Barnes	Liverpool (sub Gascoigne)
Platt	Sampdoria
Beardsley	Newcastle United (sub Barmby)
Sheringham	Tottenham
Shearer	Blackburn Rovers

Result 3-3 Sheringham, Platt, Beardsley

11 June 1995
v BRAZIL *Wembley*
Flowers	Blackburn Rovers
Neville	Manchester United
Scales	Liverpool (sub Barton)
Cooper	Nottingham Forest
Pearce	Nottingham Forest
Anderton	Tottenham
Platt	Sampdoria
Batty	Blackburn R. (sub Gascoigne)
Le Saux	Blackburn Rovers
Sheringham	Tottenham (sub Collymore)
Shearer	Blackburn Rovers

Result 1-3 Le Saux

6 September 1995
v COLOMBIA *Wembley*
Seaman	Arsenal
G. Neville	Manchester United
Le Saux	Blackburn Rovers
Howey	Newcastle United
Adams	Arsenal
Redknapp	Liverpool (sub Lee)
Gascoigne	Rangers (sub Barnes)
Wise	Chelsea
McManaman	Liverpool
Barmby	Middlesbrough
Shearer	Blackburn R. (sub Sheringham)

Result 0-0

ENGLAND INTERNATIONAL LINE-UPS AND STATISTICS 1995-96

11 October 1995
v NORWAY *Oslo*

Seaman	Arsenal
G. Neville	Manchester United
Adams	Arsenal
Pallister	Manchester United
Pearce	Nottingham Forest
Wise	Chelsea (sub Stone)
Redknapp	Liverpool
Lee	Newcastle United
Barmby	Middlesbro' (sub Sheringham)
McManaman	Liverpool
Shearer	Blackburn Rovers

Result 0-0

24 April 1996
v CROATIA *Wembley*

Seaman	Arsenal
G. Neville	Manchester United
Pearce	Nottingham Forest
Ince	Inter Milan
Wright	Liverpool
McManaman	Liverpool
Platt	Arsenal
Gascoigne	Rangers
Fowler	Liverpool
Sheringham	Tottenham Hotspur
Stone	Nottingham Forest

Result 0-0

15 November 1995
v SWITZERLAND *Wembley*

Seaman	Arsenal
G. Neville	Manchester United
Pearce	Nottingham Forest
Adams	Arsenal
Pallister	Manchester United
Lee	Newcastle United
Redknapp	Liverpool (sub Stone)
Gascoigne	Rangers
McManaman	Liverpool
Sheringham	Tottenham Hotspur
Shearer	Blackburn Rovers

Result 3-1 Pearce, Sheringham, Stone

18 May 1996
v HUNGARY *Wembley*

Seaman	Arsenal (sub Walker)
G. Neville	Manchester United
Pearce	Nottingham Forest
Wright	Liverpool (sub Southgate)
Anderton	Tottenham Hotspur
Ince	Inter Milan (sub Campbell)
Wilcox	Blackburn Rovers
Ferdinand	Newcastle Utd. (sub Shearer)
Lee	Newcastle United
Platt	Arsenal (sub Wise)
Sheringham	Tottenham Hotspur

Result 3-0 Anderton 2, Platt

27 March 1996
v BULGARIA *Wembley*

Seaman	Arsenal
G. Neville	Manchester United
Pearce	Nottingham Forest
Ince	Inter Milan
Southgate	Aston Villa
Howey	Newcastle United
McManaman	Liverpool
Gascoigne	Rangers (sub Lee)
Ferdinand	Newcastle United (sub Platt)
Sheringham	Tottenham H. (sub Fowler)
Stone	Nottingham Forest

Result 1-0 Ferdinand

23 May 1996
v CHINA *Beijing*

Flowers	Blackburn Rovers (sub Walker)
G. Neville	Manchester United
P. Neville	Manchester United
Redknapp	Liverpool
Adams	Arsenal (sub Ehiogu)
Southgate	Aston Villa
Barmby	Middlesbrough (sub Beardsley)
Gascoigne	Rangers
Shearer	Blackburn Rovers (sub Fowler)
McManaman	Liverpool (sub Stone)
Anderton	Tottenham Hotspur

Result 3-0 Barmby 2, Gascoigne

ENGLAND INTERNATIONAL LINE-UPS AND STATISTICS 1996

8 June 1996
v SWITZERLAND *Wembley*

Seaman	Arsenal
G. Neville	Manchester United
Pearce	Nottingham Forest
Ince	Inter Milan
Adams	Arsenal
Southgate	Aston Villa
Gascoigne	Rangers (sub Platt)
Shearer	Blackburn Rovers
Sheringham	Tottenham H. (sub Barmby)
Anderton	Tottenham Hotspur
McManaman	Liverpool (sub Stone)

Result 1-1 Shearer

15 June 1996
v SCOTLAND *Wembley*

Seaman	Arsenal
G. Neville	Manchester United
Pearce	Nott'm Forest (sub Redknapp (sub Campbell))
Ince	Inter Milan (sub Stone)
Adams	Arsenal
Southgate	Aston Villa
Gascoigne	Rangers
Shearer	Blackburn Rovers
Sheringham	Tottenham Hotspur
Anderton	Tottenham Hotspur
McManaman	Liverpool

Result 2-0 Shearer, Gascoigne

18 June 1996
v HOLLAND *Wembley*

Seaman	Arsenal
G. Neville	Manchester United
Adams	Arsenal
Southgate	Aston Villa
Pearce	Nottingham Forest
Gascoigne	Rangers
Ince	Inter Milan (sub Platt)
McManaman	Liverpool
Shearer	Blackburn Rvrs. (sub Barmby)
Anderton	Tottenham Hotspur
Sheringham	Tottenham H. (sub Fowler)

Result 4-1 Shearer 2 (1 pen), Sheringham 2

22 June 1996
v SPAIN *Wembley*

Seaman	Arsenal
G. Neville	Manchester United
Pearce	Nottingham Forest
Adams	Arsenal
Southgate	Aston Villa
Platt	Arsenal
Gascoigne	Rangers
Shearer	Blackburn Rovers
Sheringham	Tottenham Hotspur (sub Stone)
Anderton	Tottenham H. (sub Fowler)
McManaman	Liverpool (sub Barmby)

Result 0-0 (aet) England won 4-2 on penalties

26 June 1996
v GERMANY *Wembley*

Seaman	Arsenal
Pearce	Nottingham Forest
Ince	Inter Milan
Adams	Arsenal
Southgate	Aston Villa
Platt	Arsenal
Gascoigne	Rangers
Shearer	Blackburn Rovers
Sheringham	Tottenham Hotspur
Anderton	Tottenham Hotspur
McManaman	Liverpool

Result 1-1 (aet) Shearer
Germany won 6-5 on penalties

Our publications : –

ENGLAND INTERNATIONAL LINE-UPS AND STATISTICS 1872-1960

ENGLAND INTERNATIONAL LINE-UPS AND STATISTICS 1961-1996

are now available each priced £5.95 post free
from : –

Soccer Book Publishing Limited
72 St. Peter's Avenue
Cleethorpes
N.E. Lincolnshire
DN35 8HU

THE

25

YEAR RECORD
SERIES

Top quality 25 season histories with line-ups, results, scorers, attendances and season-by-season write-ups.

Titles currently available...

Chelsea F.C.	Seasons 1971-72 to 1995-9
Middlesbrough F.C.	Seasons 1971-72 to 1995-9
Preston North End F.C.	Seasons 1971-72 to 1995-9
Southampton F.C.	Seasons 1971-72 to 1995-9
Sunderland F.C.	Seasons 1971-72 to 1995-9
Aston Villa F.C.	Seasons 1970-71 to 1994-9
Celtic F.C.	Seasons 1970-71 to 1994-9
Derby County F.C.	Seasons 1970-71 to 1994-9
Everton F.C.	Seasons 1970-71 to 1994-9
Leeds United F.C.	Seasons 1970-71 to 1994-9
Liverpool F.C.	Seasons 1970-71 to 1994-9
Manchester United F.C.	Seasons 1970-71 to 1994-9
Newcastle United F.C.	Seasons 1970-71 to 1994-9
Nottingham Forest F.C.	Seasons 1970-71 to 1994-9
Rangers F.C.	Seasons 1970-71 to 1994-9

Also available (no write-ups):
Burnley F.C. .... Seasons 1969-70 to 1993-9

All titles are softback and priced £4.99

Available post free from:

Soccer Book Publishing Ltd. (Dept. SBP)
72 St. Peter's Avenue
Cleethorpes
N.E. Lincolnshire
DN35 8HU

Tel. (01472) 601893
Fax (01472) 698546